Drat! Mythed Again

Drat! Mythed Again

Second Thoughts on Utah

Steve Warren

Altair Publishing Company
West Valley City, Utah

Cover illustration by Marnie Sears of The Typesetter, Sandy, Utah
Cartoons by Al Lediard of Bailey-Montague & Associates, Salt Lake City

ISBN 0-938117-02-05
Library of Congress Catalog Card No. 86-81186

Altair Publishing Company
P.O. Box 20024
West Valley City, Utah 84120

Contents

Introduction

In 1984, New York writers Christopher Cerf and Victor Navasky produced a volume of authoritative misinformation entitled *The Experts Speak*. I enjoyed their book.

Nevertheless, I felt *The Experts Speak* had one major flaw — its 391 pages contained not a single reference to Utah, nor to the Great Basin, nor to the Mormon Church, nor even, as far as I could tell, to any prominent person in Utah history.

Drat! Mythed Again corrects this gross oversight. Its pages contain not a single reference *without* a Utah connection.

Its purpose is to entertain.

Still, I am aware that some, like the Provo resident who answered "sounds deplorable!" to a survey about the book, will not be entertained.

To those who feel entertainment alone is insufficient reason to delve into the world of Utah miscalculations, I'll toss in this thought: a little healthy skepticism never hurt anyone. After all, some national publications have recently assigned to Utah a high gullibility quotient. They have branded the state "the fraud capital of the nation," and the "sewer of the securities industry," and have asked, "What makes the folks in Utah so gullible?" These somewhat exaggerated comments spring, of course, from the numerous scams which thrive in the Beehive State.

But *Drat! Mythed Again* is also for optimists. It demonstrates that great successes can be achieved by those wise enough to recognize false expertise.

It may appear that certain Utahns, cited often on these pages, chronically misfire. On the contrary, their quotability may simply reflect a willingness to speak without equivocation on issues. In an era in which wishy-washiness has become an art form, thank goodness for those willing to take stands or to make unqualified predictions.

The reader will also note herein many more quotes attributed to and more miscalculations made by the *Salt Lake Tribune* than by other Utah newspapers. Does this mean that the *Tribune* goofs more than other papers? Not necessarily. I generally used the *Tribune* as a first newspaper source because the *Tribune's* yearly name and subject index, published by the paper for decades, facilitated my research. I compliment the *Tribune* for compiling this index.

Finally, this is a book of highlights, arbitrarily selected. For every item included, many others have been omitted or (I admit it) overlooked. Certain material has not been included simply to avoid repetition of genres already covered. In the interest of balance, I have tried to select a broad range of material, letting the chips fall where they may, regardless of my own political, religious, or personal sentiments. Naturally, the reader will ultimately judge whether I have succeeded.

Steve Warren

Part 1

Places Great and Small

Chapter 1

The Great Basin

Early Assessments

"A region whose uses are unimaginable, unless to hold the rest of the globe together, or to teach patience to travelers."[1]

—Samuel Bowles
   (editor of the Hartford Times*)*

"This region is doomed to perpetual sterility."[2]

—T. J. Farnham
   (explorer, lawyer)

"Let the Mormons have the territory to themselves — it is worth very little to others."[3]

—Horace Greeley
   (editor of the New York Tribune*)*

"As the emigrants saw it, this was a country that God forgot."[4]

—Herbert E. Bolton
   (American historian)

"What do we want with that vast worthless area, that region of savages and wild beasts, of deserts, of shifting sands and whirlwinds of dust, of cactus and prairie dogs? To what use could we ever hope to put those great deserts, those endless mountain ranges, impenetrable and covered to their bases with eternal snow?"[5]

—Daniel Webster
  (lawyer, statesman),
  evaluating the West

 Utah's "worthless" mountain ranges now generate $350 million annually in ski revenue.

"Of the entire country between the Missouri River and California, a traveler who crossed it in 1851 wrote: 'it is of no account; the soil is poor, sandy, and too dry to produce anything but this little short grass, and, when it does rain, in three hours afterward you could not tell that it had rained at all.' "[6]

—in *Kingdom of the Saints*

Salt Lake Valley

"The saints could not possibly subsist in the Great Salt Lake Valley, as according to the testimony of the mountaineers, it froze there every month in the year, and the ground was too dry to sprout seeds without irrigation, and irrigated with the cold mountain streams the seeds planted would be chilled and prevented from growing."[7]

—Samuel Brannan
(pioneer, newspaperman)

(The preceding is one pioneer's recollection of Brannan's comments to Brigham Young. After hearing this opinion, Young laughed and made some rather insignificant remark, said Brannan, "but when he has fairly tried it, he will find that I was right and he was wrong, and will come to California."[8]

Brannan was not the first to recommend emigration to California. Illinois governor Thomas Ford, who knew of Brigham Young's desire to settle in a region no one else wanted, in 1845 urged the pioneers to settle California: "You would remain there a long time before you would be disturbed by the proximity of other settlements."[9] Four years later, California was overrun by the gold rush.)

"A broad and barren plain hemmed in by mountains, blistering in the burning rays of the mid-summer sun. No waving fields, no swaying forests, no verdant meadows to refresh the weary eye, but on all sides a seemingly interminable waste of sagebrush bespangled with sunflowers — the paradise of the lizard, the cricket, and the rattlesnake."[10]

—Orson F. Whitney
(Mormon writer)

"Mr. Young, I would give a thousand dollars, if I knew that an ear of corn could be ripened in these mountains. I have been here twenty years, and have tried it in vain, over and over again."[11]

—Jim Bridger
 (explorer, scout),
 advising Brigham Young
 to settle elsewhere

Taming the Desert

Not long after the arrival of the Utah pioneers, it became clear that the region was not to be "doomed to perpetual sterility." But this has given rise to what some consider to be a myth of equal proportions — that the pioneers tamed a barren, unhospitable wasteland. In fact, says Wallace Stegner in *Mormon Country,* the pioneers simply settled in the fertile, watered valleys and left the rest of the region alone.

"Most of those who gazed on Salt Lake Valley in 1847 had the same initial impression: fertile soil, good vegetation, a generally favorable climate, plenty of timber in the mountains, abundant water in the mountain streams, and a place that promised golden opportunity for agricultural success."[12]

— Thomas G. Alexander and James B. Allen
 (historians)

"We gazed with wonder and admiration upon the vast, rich fertile valley which lay for about twenty-five miles in length and 16 miles in width, clothed with the heaviest garb of green vegetation...a glorious valley abounding with the best fresh water springs, riverlets, creeks, brooks and rivers...the grandest and most sublime scenery that could be obtained on the globe."[13]

—Wilford Woodruff
 (Mormon pioneer, apostle),
 describing pioneer entrance into
 Salt Lake Valley

Gold Everywhere!

"The undersigned has abundant reason to know that the mountains of Utah, north, south, east, and west, are prolific in mineral wealth. Gold, silver, iron, copper, lead, and coal are found in almost every direction, in quantities which promise the richest results to the adventurous explorer and the industrious miner."[14]

—General Patrick E. Connor
March 1, 1864

"Gold in the mountains! Gold in the rocks!! Gold in the sands!!! Gold in the steams!!!! Gold in the kanyons!!!!! Gold in the cellars!!!!!! Gold in the streets!!!!!!! Gold in the gutters!!!!!!!! Gold everywhere!!!!!!!!!

"But stop, we wish the public to know things as they are. In sober earnest and truth, where is all this Gold? We presume, from what we hear, that it is still tolerable plenty in California, very plenty in Washington, Idaho and Arizona Territories, and that there is some in Colorado and Nevada Territories. But, so far as Utah is concerned, after sifting all reports to the present date, it is only in the hands of Madam Rumor, who is lavishing her blandishments and loudly blowing her trumpet to deceive the thoughtless into a waste of their time and means."

—Editorial,
Deseret News,
March 2, 1864

Odd Creatures in the Desert

Portrayals of the Great Basin as unfit for human habitation undoubtedly helped give rise to mythological animal life such as the Salt Lake monster, a bellowing, aquatic beast given to attacking campers near Great Salt Lake.

An Easterner wrote a local official to inquire whether there are bullfrogs "in your Utah deserts seven years old who have never learned to swim?"[15] (But that was more than a century ago. Now Utah has rabbits four years old who have never stopped running from the rising Great Salt Lake.)

Another strange creature was the salt bear:

Salt bears are pure white and invisible against their stark background; you can see them only when their shiny little black eyes are open and look straight at you; the salt bears are responsible, we are told, for tearing up the highways crossing the salt flats.[16]

NOTES FOR CHAPTER 1

1. Leonard Arrington, *Great Basin Kingdom,* 1958, p. 43.
2. Frank K. Seegmiller, "The Economic Value of the Natural Resources of the Great Basin According to the Writings of Early Travelers and Explorers," masters thesis, University of Utah, 1923, p. 2.
3. Horace Greeley, *An Overland Journey from New York to San Francisco,* 1860.
4. Milton R. Hunter, *Brigham Young the Colonizer,* 1941, p. 29.
5. Jan Harold Brunvand, *Studies in Western Folklore and Fiction,* 1972, p. 3.
6. Ray B. West, *Kingdom of the Saints,* 1957, p. 182.
7. Richard D. Poll, Thomas G. Alexander, Eugene E. Campell, David E. Miller, *Utah's History,* 1978, p. 116.
8. Ibid.
9. Leland Hargrave Creer, *Founding of an Empire,* 1947, p. 224.
10. Thomas G. Alexander and James B. Allen, *Mormons and Gentiles,* 1984, p. 23.
11. *Journal of Discourses,* Vol. 8, p. 288.
12. Alexander and Allen, p. 23.
13. B. H. Roberts, *Comprehensive History of the Church,* 1930, p. 231.
14. House of Representatives, 55th Congress, 1st Session, Doc. No. 59, Part 2, 1897, p. 774.
15. Brunvand, p. 4.
16. Ibid.

Chapter 2

Great Salt Lake

Who discovered Great Salt Lake? How big was the lake? How high will the lake rise? When it comes to confounding historians, weathermen, resort developers, and politicians, Great Salt Lake is in a league by itself.

Who Discovered the Lake?

Jim Bridger

"James Bridger was the first discoverer of Great Salt Lake."[1]

—Robert Campbell
(Canadian trader, explorer)

Captain John H. Weber

"The Captain told me more than once of his discovery of Salt Lake in 1823. He called it a great boon to them, as salt was plentiful around the border of the lake and for some time before they had used gunpowder on their meat, which was principally buffalo."[2]

—J.C. Hughey,
in 1897 letter to
Salt Lake Tribune

Etienne Provost

"It was visited in 1824 by Etienne Provost, and in the following year by James Bridger, famous scout and trailmaker."[3]

—*Literary Digest*

Wilson Price Hunt

"Perhaps the first white men to visit the Great Salt Lake region was a detachment of four men from the party of trappers under Wilson Price Hunt who in 1812 were making their way from St. Louis to Astoria while in the employ of John Jacob Astor's Pacific Fur Company...If their narrative be true, it is likely that they were the first white men to explore the Bear River to its affluence with the Great Salt Lake."[4]

—in *Founding of an Empire*

Mr. Miller

"A Mr. Miller, of the Jacob Astor party, stood by its shore in 1820."[5]

—in *Our Inland Sea*

Louis Vasquez

"Descending Bear River, the story went, Vasquez in company with several others rode into Great Salt Lake Valley and so discovered the lake, at first taking it to be an arm of the Pacific."[6]

—in *Great Salt Lake*

Historians now generally credit Jim Bridger with discovering the lake in 1824. But Bridger, at the moment of discovery, wasn't so sure: "Hell," he snorted, "We are on the shores of the Pacific."[7]

A Terrible Whirlpool

Several mountain men "were firmly convinced that somewhere on the surface of the lake was a terrible whirlpool, through which the lake waters found their way to the ocean by subterranean passage,"[8] said historian Dale Morgan.

In 1870, boatmen from Corinne, making regular runs on the lake, supposedly saw a hole off Fremont Island into which the lake was rushing. One report said: "A schooner last Tuesday was almost drawn into it."[9]

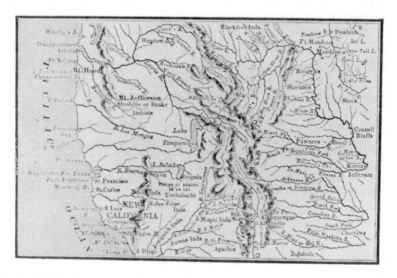

Finley's 1826 map (above) shows Great Salt Lake (L. Salado) south of Lake Timpanogos (Utah Lake). It is drained by a single river, R. Buenaventura, flowing to San Francisco. The John Harris 1705 map depicts Great Salt Lake as "The Great Lake of Thongo," with two river outlets extending to the Pacific. Notice the island of California.

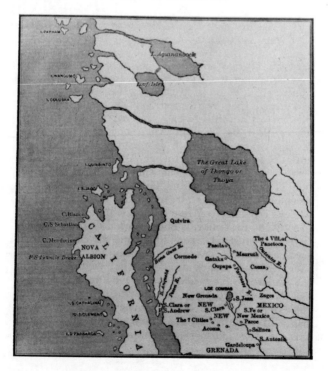

Circumference of the Lake

By the late 1820s, the existence of a large body of salt water was well-established. Determining its size was another matter.

"It is about two hundred and fifty miles in circumference."[10]

—Joseph Williams
(Methodist minister, explorer)

"It is about 400 miles in circumference."[11]

—Daniel Potts
(explorer)

"It was 550 miles around it."[12]

—Jim Bridger
(explorer, scout)

The Fall and Rise of Great Salt Lake

Note: In May 1986 the rapidly rising lake exceeded its historic high of 4211.6 feet. The alarming rise prompted the state legislature to approve a west desert pumping project to increase evaporation.

"The next ten years will witness its shrinkage, for lack of affluent water, to a size smaller than has before been observed...Antelope, Stansbury, Carrington, Hat, and Dolphin islands will be permanently united to the land."[13]

—Grove Karl Gilbert
(geologist),
1890

"The opinion now almost universally prevails among scientists that this mysterious body of water...is certain within the course of a century to disappear from the map. Some scientists who have made a careful study of the fluctuations of the lake for the past several years, even declare that it will be dried up within a quarter of a century...Statistics indicate that Great Salt Lake, the Dead Sea of America, is doomed — that it is gradually drying up."[14]

—*Scientific American*
  July 2, 1904

(These statements in *Scientific American* were "so well-founded," said the author of the article, "that the predicted destiny of the lake can not well be disputed.")

"Huge loss of lake water by evaporation" has caused great alarm among lake watchers. Construction of a dike around the south half of the lake was proposed in an effort to reduce the surface area exposed to evaporation.

—*Denver Post*
  August 21, 1966

"The lake will not dry up nor rise above its historically high level of 1873."[15]

—Ted Arnow
  (Utah District Chief, Water Resources
  Division of the U.S. Geological Survey),
  February 6, 1979

"There is one chance in 100 of the lake high in 1985 reaching 4204.03 feet, the most likely level is 4199.03 feet."[16]

—Utah Water Research Laboratory
  1981

"[Stan Elmer] predicted the lake would continue to fall as it had done since 1976, with only intermittent rises to temporary peaks."

—*Utah Holiday*
  July 1983
  (Stan Elmer is lands planner with Utah's
  Division of State Lands and Forestry.)

"The chance of the lake rising above 4203.4 feet over the long term is only 15 percent."[17]

—Paul Summers
*(assistant planning director, Utah
State Division of Water Resources),
1983*

"There is an 85 percent chance that the Great Salt Lake high water level will reach the 4,212.5-foot elevation by June 1985."[18]

—Dale R. Hawkins
*(professor of finance at Weber State),
February 1985*

 The 1985 peak was 4209.95 feet.

NOTES FOR CHAPTER 2

1. Leland Hargrave Creer, *Founding of an Empire,* 1947, p. 48.
2. *Salt Lake Tribune,* July 4, 1897, letter from J.C. Hughey of Bellevue, Iowa.
3. *Literary Digest,* October 19, 1935.
4. Creer, p. 44.
5. Alfred Lambourne, *Our Inland Sea,* 1909, from the introduction.
6. Dale Morgan, *The Great Salt Lake,* 1947, p. 70.
7. Ibid.
8. Ibid., p. 138.
9. David E. Miller, "The Great Salt Lake," in *Utah Historical Quarterly,* July 1959, p. 298.
10. Joseph Williams journal, cited in Morgan, *The Great Salt Lake,* p. 132.
11. Philadelphia *Gazette and Public Advertiser,* November 14, 1826, cited in Morgan, *The Great Salt Lake,* p. 82.
12. Morgan, p. 81. This estimate is based on reports Bridger received from his men.
13. Grove Karl Gilbert, Monographs of the U.S. Geological Survey, Lake Bonneville, 1890, pp. 250, 251.
14. *Scientific American,* July 2, 1904, p. 9.
15. *Tribune,* February 7, 1979.
16. Utah Water Research Laboratory, "Update on Estimation of Water Surface Elevation Probabilities for the Great Salt Lake," February 1981, Utah State University.
17. *Tribune,* January 19, 1983.
18. *Deseret News,* February 10, 1985.

Chapter 3

Cities, Towns and Buildings

Salt Lake City

"[Salt Lake City is] a more gloomy place than Ogden itself...Daily in the many stores of that decaying city can be seen the merchant vacantly staring at the deserted street, and behind each counter the idle salesman doing the monotonous duty of a statue...like other rural towns, [Salt Lake City] will have to come to the marts of trade for her wares. To Corinne the merchants of Zion are invited."

—*Utah Reporter*
 May 24, 1870

"A community of traitors, murderers, fanatics, and whores."[1]

—General Patrick E. Connor
 1862

"[In Salt Lake City] rush-hour traffic is something you hear happens in Denver."

—*Forbes*
 June 20, 1983

Ogden

"[Ogden is] a drowsy place...a village more stupid than Sleepy Hollow."

—*Utah Reporter*
  May 24, 1870

"People in Ogden don't seem to give a damn about anything."[2]

—Salt Lake City TV newsman
  1975

 Not long ago Ogden was considered a second-rate city. But if numerous civic awards received over the past ten years are any indication, Ogden has become one of the most progressive and livable cities in the west.

Lincoln

"Business is lively and all signs point to permanent prosperity."[3]

—Salt Lake newspaper reporter
  1862

 Lincoln is a long-forgotten mining camp located in southwestern Utah.

Mosida

"Mosida-by-the-lake, a beautiful spot where the land is rich and opportunity beckons!"[4]

—Advertisement,
  Mosida Fruit Lands Company
  1910

 Mosida, an agricultural boom town located on the southwest shores of Utah Lake, became a ghost town after the lake level dropped in 1915 leaving the town's pumps high and dry.

Silver Reef

"Geologists and engineers all agreed that silver couldn't be found in sandstone."[5]

—in *Some Dreams Die*
   1874

They soon changed their minds. Estimates of how much money was generated from ore in sandstone at Silver Reef in southern Utah reached $20 million based on turn-of-the-century monetary values.

South Salt Lake

"We don't annex swamps."[6]

—Salt Lake City government
   1938

This, in effect, was Salt Lake City's response to requests by residents of the South Salt Lake area to be annexed by Salt Lake City. When Salt Lake City rejected the requests on grounds that services provided to the swampy area simply wouldn't be worth the small tax revenue returned, South Salt Lake made itself a city in 1938.

Times have changed. South Salt Lake now ranks fifth among Utah cities in gross sales tax revenue produced even though the city is only the 23rd largest in the state. Recent comparisons of tax levies, and water and sewer rates on a $75,000 home show Salt Lake City property owners pay two and one half times more than South Salt Lakers. Now, adjoining areas are petitioning to be annexed by South Salt Lake.

Salt Lake City should have known better. After all, before heading west, the eventual settlers of Utah had created the city of Nauvoo, Illinois, from a swamp.

Bloomington

"The old-timers...couldn't conceive that the area would ever be more than a place to farm."[7]

—*St. George* magazine

Bloomington, now one of Utah's fastest growing communities, has become a popular setting for retirees and families young and old. It has been promoted as the "Palm Springs of Utah."

Corinne

Perhaps no city in Utah history has ever held a higher opinion of itself than did Corinne in the late 1860s and in the 1870s. Exaggerated claims printed in Corinne's *Utah Reporter* were often taken at face value outside the state. By 1880, however, the "burg on the Bear" turned out to be a bear of a burg as population plummeted from several thousand to only 277.

"[Corinne is] a city of permanent importance...a permanent, well-governed city."[8]

—*Cincinnati Commercial*
  October 17, 1868

"[Corinne has] better prospects for growth than Ogden."[9]

—*New York Herald*
  December 29, 1869

"Our growth and progress to the present time presents remarkable evidence of permanence and stability...the foundations of a great city are fixed here."

—*Utah Reporter*
  April 7, 1870

"This is the emporium of the hills...as firmly as she is fixed at the gate of the mountains so surely will Corinne retain her metropolitan character."

—*Utah Reporter*
  May 24, 1870

"Corinne is even now entering a career of unprecedented prosperity...
her best days are yet to come...Its inhabitants remain hopeful and
confident, and a brighter day already seems dawning."[10]

—*New York Times*
July 20, 1878

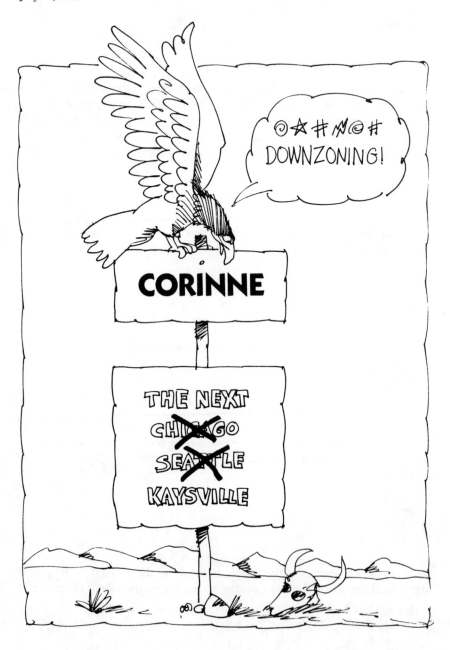

Corinne was not reluctant to compare herself with more prominent cities:

> Corinne — the coming Chicago of the Great Salt Lake Basin.[11]

> Today the streets wore the look of a second New York, filled with businessmen and produce dealers.[12]

> Seattle may be a very "prosperous" town for the "web foot" country, but it's not what we call a prosperous town on the line of the great transcontinental.[13]

The city of Corinne produced a promotional brochure in 1875 that gave many reasons for settling there:

> Summer nights always cool...The climate effectually cures asthma ...consumption is cured in all its earliest stages, and is not produced in the climate, it being above "the Tubercial Zone"... No Winter feed is required, sheep and cattle subsisting on the native grasses, and looking better in the Spring than the hay-fed cattle of the Eastern States.[14]

Thistle

For decades Mormon residents of Thistle joined in singing a favorite Mormon hymn, "Firm as the Mountains Around Us." But in 1983, the singing stopped. In mid-April the Thistle area was hit by a huge mountain-slide described in one news account as

> an entire mountain sliding downhill...the mountain, sliding on the wet clay as if it were on a greased cookie sheet, is moving down the east side of the canyon over the streambed, railroad tracks and roadway until it hits the solid rock-west wall of the canyon.[15]

The mudslide formed a natural dam, water backed up, and Thistle became Thistle Lake. It took until December 30 to reopen U.S. Highway 6 through the canyon.

The Thistle slide, according to U.S. Forest Service geologist Earl P. Olson, is the sixth largest landslide of the century in the United States.

The 1983 Thistle mountainslide.

The Twelve-Mile Canyon slide of 1983 ranks fifth, and the Cottonwood slide in Manti Canyon in 1975-76 is fourth. Farmington is also the site of an historic landslide of massive proportions. Other landslides have occurred in City Creek Canyon and in the Washington Terrace area of Weber County.

In its August 1983 issue, *Utah Holiday* gave "Firm as the Mountains Around Us" the distinction "worst local favorite hymn to sing in Utah in 1983." Second worst went to "For the Strength of the Hills We Bless Thee."

In the Church's 1985 hymnal, the title, "Firm as the Mountains Around Us," was changed to "Carry On," which is exactly what former Thistle residents had to do after the disaster.

West Valley City

In 1980, residents of the unincorporated Granger-Hunter-Redwood area of Salt Lake County voted by a narrow margin to incorporate, thereby creating West Valley City. Six years after incorporation, property taxes on a $75,000 home in West Valley City are about $40 less than the same home in the unincorporated area of Salt Lake County.[16] Now, residents seldom discuss the past county government. They have grown accustomed to higher service levels and greater accessibility provided by the new city government.

Plans have been made to construct a new city hall in West Valley. Instead of following the examples of Salt Lake County and Salt Lake City of incurring high finance costs associated with bonding, West Valley has saved the $5.5 million needed to pay for its building. It is precisely this kind of financial planning which recently brought West Valley a prestigious award for outstanding budgetary practices. Only 41 other U.S. cities have received such recognition.[17]

According to experts, West Valley City had almost no chance of turning out so well. Following is a chronological look at the birth of West Valley. It is based on newspaper accounts.

July 14, 1979

Studies by Salt Lake County show taxes on a $50,000 home in the proposed West Valley City would increase by $156 to $186 to pay for municipal services.[18]

February 3, 1980

A $38,000 study prepared by John Short and Associates said the proposed city would be hit with a healthy tax increase. Opponents have pointed out that the area to be incorporated has been somewhat subsidized by the county in the past because it has only one fifth of the county tax-base but one fourth of the county population.[19]

February 24

A brochure prepared by opponents of West Valley asks area voters if they wanted to gamble their homes on less than excellent fire protection. Entitled "No Free Lunch," the brochure predicts incorporation will mean a stiff tax increase.[20]

A *Salt Lake Tribune* editorial urged West Valley voters to look closely at the price tag: "What starts cheaply generally ends up as a very costly way of doing the community's business."

Incorporation foe Bart Barker, chairman of the No Free Lunch Committee, said, "Incorporation would create a new level of bureaucracy. We can't afford that. We'd be paying city taxes on top of county taxes."[21]

February 26

Incorporation narrowly passes. The vote is 5193 to 5107.

April 3

Opponents of West Valley City have launched a disincorporation drive. K. T. Magnusson, head of Citizens for Disincorporation, says the drive appears headed for "overwhelming success... People are grabbing the petitions out of our volunteers' hands to sign them — even before they finish asking for the signatures." Magnusson said his petition carriers are collecting eleven signatures for every person that refuses to sign "and that is in districts that voted *for* incorporation!"[22]

May 8

Mayor-elect Hank Price said today that the man chosen to be West Valley's police chief has withdrawn because of the threat of disincorporation.[23]

July 7

Under the headline, "Tuesday's Disincorporation Vote Should End West Valley City," a *Salt Lake Tribune* editorial encouraged voters "to set things straight by disincorporating the infant city which should never have been created in the first place." Events since incorporation have confirmed many of the negative predictions about the city, said the *Tribune: "West Valley City should be smothered in its creaking crib before hallowed good government concepts are further outraged."*[24]

The Utah Taxpayers Association said, "Despite promises from city officials that West Valley will provide better services at a lower cost, taxpayers should expect higher taxes." The Association predicted that property taxes would nearly double.[25]

On July 8, West Valley City residents, in a 9,239 to 6,542 landslide, voted to remain a city.

Estrella Del Mar

What? Estrella Del Mar (Star of the Sea) in Utah?

Although not located in Utah, Estrella Del Mar has been of considerable interest to a number of Utahns. It was a Mexican "asset" held by Independent Clearing House and used as a lure for investors in a Ponzi scheme, said *Forbes* on June 20, 1983. Many Utah investors were told that this asset was a condominium community worth over $100 million. Clearing House promotional literature called it "some of the choicest remaining beachfront property on the North American Continent."

 A bankruptcy trustee who visited this "Jewel of the Sea of Cortez" in 1983 learned that it consisted of half-built, shoddily constructed shacks surrounded by a virtual wasteland. The area had been abandoned six years earlier.

Lamoreaux Building

Historic preservationists in Salt Lake City were happy on January 27, 1966, to read in their morning paper, "City to Save Lamoreaux Building."[26]

 Located at 415 South 200 East, the building was torn down about a year later.

Coalville Tabernacle

On March 2, 1971, Summit Stake President Reed Brown informed newsmen that, due to the controversy over the proposed demolition of the Coalville tabernacle, local LDS leaders had decided to "let things cool off for a while."[27] Opponents of the demolition, obviously pleased with the delay, announced they would continue to try to save the historic tabernacle by seeking a restraining order later in the week.

 LDS officials had a sudden change of heart, however, and demolition commenced at 5 a.m. on March 3 before a restraining order could be obtained.

Newhouse Hotel

"Newhouse Hotel Due Expansion" proclaimed a December 13, 1972, newspaper headline. The news account described plans by a Salt Lake City firm to spend $6 million to restore the downtown landmark "to its former luster."[28]

On August 10, 1978, the 15-story building was added to the National Historic Register.

 The Newhouse was demolished on June 26, 1983.

Eagle Gate

"Eagle Gate Spared," reported *Sunstone Review* in its January-February 1982 issue. "The historic Eagle Gate Apartments in downtown Salt Lake City will be renovated and preserved as an apartment complex."

 Soon thereafter it was determined the building was too crumbly to be restored. It has since been razed and replaced with a new building.

Hogle Mansion

"Hogle Mansion Gets New Lease on Life" announced a September 24, 1967, *Salt Lake Tribune* headline. The building was to be renovated and landscaped with turn-of-the-century flavor.

 Instead of lasting until the next turn of the century, the mansion's "lease on life" was extended only about a decade. It was located at 548 East South Temple.

OSHA Building

On September 23, 1978, a huge section of the roof of a building at Research Park in Salt Lake City collapsed, causing $100,000 in damage. The building was occupied by OSHA, the Occupational Safety and Health Administration.[29]

NOTES FOR CHAPTER 3

1. Dale Morgan, *The Great Salt Lake,* 1947, p. 284.
2. *Utah Holiday,* March 3, 1975.
3. George A. Thompson, *Some Dreams Die,* 1982, p. 126.
4. Raymond Duane Steele, *Goshen Valley History,* 1960, p. 169.
5. Thompson, p. 26.
6. Based on *Deseret News* article of February 16, 1986.
7. *St. George* magazine, Spring 1984.
8. Cited in Brigham D. Madsen, *Corinne: The Gentile Capital of Utah,* 1980, p. 5.
9. Ibid., p. 22.
10. Cited in *Salt Lake Daily Tribune,* July 20, 1878.
11. *Utah Reporter,* March 3, 1870.
12. *Corinne Record,* March 19, 1877.
13. *Utah Reporter,* September 29, 1870.
14. "Corinne and the Bear River Valley," promotional brochure, 1875. (A copy of this brochure is in the Western Americana collection at the University of Utah Marriott Library.)
15. *Salt Lake Tribune,* April 18, 1983.
16. From information sheet, "We did it!," by West Valley City, July 1, 1985.
17. *Deseret News,* January 2, 1985.
18. *Tribune,* July 14, 1979.
19. Ibid., February 3, 1980.
20. Ibid., February 24, 1980.
21. Ibid.
22. *Deseret News,* April 3, 1980.
23. Ibid., May 8, 1980.
24. *Tribune,* July 7, 1980, editorial.
25. Ibid., July 8, 1980.
26. Ibid., January 27, 1966.
27. *Deseret News,* March 2, 1971.
28. *Tribune,* December 13, 1972.
29. Ibid., January 5, 1979.

Part 2

Politics and Government

Chapter 4

Pols and Polls

J. Bracken Lee

Perhaps no other politician in Utah history has confounded the experts as often as J. Bracken Lee.

In the 1948 gubernatorial campaign, Governor Herbert Maw charged that if Lee were elected, liquor by the drink would become commonplace in Utah:

> Liquor by the drink can be had at this time in two ways — by an act of the legislature or by electing a governor who will eliminate the State Liquor Police Force and close his eyes to law enforcement. The underworld is not interested in the first method.[1]

 Although Lee won the election, Utah has never approved liquor by the drink.

A *Life* magazine feature on Lee on May 1, 1950, "Politician Without A Future," called Lee "a self-doomed man."

 Twenty-two years later, this man "without a future" was still in office — as mayor of Salt Lake City.

Life quoted Utah Democratic Chairman Grant Macfarland as saying the election of Lee in 1948 was the "best thing that could happen to us!" Macfarland called Lee "the Pied Piper of Price; whose pipes will soon be playing Going Home." (Lee's response: "That was a compliment. You will remember it was the Pied Piper that got rid of the rats.")

 Instead of "going home," Lee was reelected in 1952.

On January 11, 1954, *Time* attacked Lee's unwillingness to spend more on education in Utah: "The number of teachers graduating from the state's teacher's colleges has been dropping at the rate of about 200 a year." This was an incredible statistic, Lee pointed out, since Utah had no teachers' colleges.

Lee continued to fool the forecasters as mayor of Salt Lake City. Harry Jones of the *Deseret News* predicted on January 1, 1970, that Lee "will seek still another term as mayor of our beautiful City of Salt."

 Lee called it quits in 1972.

In a subhead to its July 8, 1950, article, "Lee of Utah — Champ or Scamp?," *New Leader* declared, "The Salt Lake State's cover-boy governor isn't quite the angel he's made out to be." Unwittingly, the magazine proved to be right, but for the wrong reason — its "Lee" photo wasn't the governor at all; it was Adam S. Bennion (below left), a member of the University of Utah Board of Regents. Lee, the genuine product, is on the right. A *New Leader* photo in the same article also confused the Salt Lake Temple with the tabernacle.

A DARLING of conservative national magazines is Utah's first-term Republican Governor, economizing J. Bracken Lee.

Lee himself misfired occasionally. "No honest man would want more than one term as governor," he said while campaigning against incumbent Governor Herbert Maw in 1948.[2]

 In 1952, Lee was reelected governor of Utah, and in 1956 he tried unsuccessfully for a third term.

In 1956, in spite of President Eisenhower's announced intention to seek reelection, Lee said, "I do not believe Mr. Eisenhower will run again."[3]

 Ike was reelected by a wide margin later in the year.

Ezra Taft Benson

In January 1961, when President Eisenhower left office, only two men remained from his original 1953 cabinet: Postmaster General Art Summerfield and Ezra Taft Benson, Secretary of Agriculture. The most remarkable aspect of Secretary Benson's extraordinary staying power was that throughout his tenure, political experts had consistently predicted Benson was "on the way out."

February 17, 1953

A White House aide, quoted in a national column, says "Benson is expendable" and might be made an ambassador.[4]

September 16, 1953

The agricultural panel of the National Democratic Committee predicted that the welfare of the farmer "will be a major political factor in the defeat of the Republicans in 1954 and 1956."[5] The following day, newspapers reported that Secretary Benson, thought to be a political liability for President Eisenhower, "would be succeeded by Gov. Dan Thornton of Colorado, a close friend and golf companion of the President."[6]

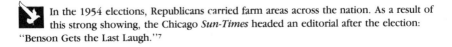 In the 1954 elections, Republicans carried farm areas across the nation. As a result of this strong showing, the Chicago *Sun-Times* headed an editorial after the election: "Benson Gets the Last Laugh."[7]

February 1958

Forty GOP House members from Midwestern states held a closed door meeting concerning Secretary Benson's policy of lowering agricultural price supports. The group called for Benson's resignation. Otherwise, they would "plow him under."[8]

Representative A. L. Miller of Nebraska said, "If Benson remains in office, it will mean the loss of 20 or 25 Republican House seats in the Midwest."

"He's the best weapon the Democrats have," Miller added.[9]

Another Republican congressman was so concerned that he pleaded with Meade Alcorn, the Republican National chairman: "Whatever you do, don't let that so-and-so Benson into my district this year."[10]

 Later in 1958 the picture had changed so dramatically that the same congressman said, "I wish you would do everything you can to get Ezra Benson into my district this fall."[11] At about the same time, columnist Roscoe Drummond observed:

> Mr. Benson has emerged as the most influential member of the Eisenhower cabinet, as the most secure figure in the Eisenhower administration. And now, improbable as it may have seemed when numerous Republican politicians were trying to hound him out of office, as one of the most politically popular spokesmen in government.[12]

William Dawson

John Snow, chairman of the Dawson for Congress Committee, predicted on November 3, 1958, that "the great majority" will vote to reelect Representative Dawson. Snow said the only thing that could beat Dawson would be a light voter turnout.[13]

 Two days later, in a record off-year voter turnout, Dawson was defeated by David S. King.

Arthur V. Watkins

Political analysts had a bad year in 1958. On October 23, the *Deseret News* reported Senator Watkins is "solidifying his slim lead. "Even the

Democrats concede he [Frank Moss] may have still some distance to go to even avoid finishing third.''[14]

A week later the *News* observed: "In every instance, Sen. Arthur V. Watkins is seen leading the field in his bid for re-election, followed by Independent J. Bracken Lee and Democrat Frank E. Moss.''[15]

A Lee ad of November 2, addressed "To All Good Democrats," concluded, "Mr. Moss obviously has lost favor with the voters.''[16]

On election eve, President Eisenhower was quoted in a Watkins newspaper ad as predicting the voters of Utah would "overwhelmingly" support Watkins on election day.[17]

 Moss won with 38 percent. Watkins had 34.8; Lee 26.4.

Calvin L. Rampton

In the 1964 Democratic gubernatorial primary, Calvin L. Rampton was branded a "loser" by his opponent, Ernest H. Dean. Dean ran this ad the day before the primary:

★ **WHO'S INTEREST IS FOR ALL THE PEOPLE?**

★ # ERNEST H. DEAN'S

★

★ ERNEST H. DEAN'S RECORD | CAL RAMPTON'S RECORD

★ **WINNER** | **LOSER**

★ He has led his ticket in every election.	★ 1950 election for State Senate	**DEFEATED**
★ He has won four state Legislative elections.	★ 1952 Election for State Chairman	**DEFEATED**
★ He was elected by his fellow legislators in three successive sessions to: Majority Leader - Minority Leader - Speaker of the House - Chairman of the Legislative Council.	★ 1954 Election for State Senate	**DEFEATED**
	★ 1960 Election for State Committeeman	**DEFEATED**
	★ 1962 Election for U.S. Senate	**DEFEATED**

★ **WHO WINS ELECTIONS?**

★ # ERNEST H. DEAN DOES!

 Rampton trounced Dean by a 62-38 percent margin.

Rampton recalls that in the 1964 campaign he had to run, not only against other candidates, but against his own two-syllable surname:

> The myth was that no governor of Utah whose last name contained more than one syllable could be elected to a second term. Indeed, up until 1968 history seemed to bear this out. Of the first five governors of Utah, three, Cutler, Bamberger, and Mabey, were one-term governors while the two whose names contained only one syllable, Wells and Spry, were re-elected. There followed five governors, Dern, Blood, Maw, Clyde, and Lee, all of them having single-syllable last names, and all of whom were elected to a second term.
>
> In the 1964 primary, my primary opponent had a last name containing a single syllable. There were actually circulars distributed during that primary campaign telling Democrats that if they wanted to hold the governorship for more than a single term, they should not nominate a candidate with a multi-syllable last name. Fotunately for me, the myth did not have a great effect on the campaign.[18]

 Rampton became Utah's only three-term governor. His three-syllable successor, Matheson, was elected to a second term. The Republicans, in choosing Norm Bangerter as their 1984 nominee, also ignored the myth.

The current "reality" of Utah politics is that successful gubernatorial candidates must have surnames of two or more syllables.

Ernest Wilkinson

In its August 21, 1964, issue, *Time* gave this forecast on the Ernest Wilkinson-Ted Moss Senate race: "The way things stand now, Wilkinson can start packing to move back to Washington."

 Moss won 57 percent of the vote.

Wallace F. Bennett

Speaking at a Lincoln Day Rally in Thermopolis, Wyoming, on February 12, 1964, Senator Wallace F. Bennett predicted that President

Johnson will be unable to maintain his present popularity or translate it into votes "once flesh and blood opposition is in the field against him."[19]

 Johnson carried 61 percent of the popular vote against Barry Goldwater in November 1964, a 20th century record.

Richard M. Nixon

In a November 5, 1972, editorial, the *Salt Lake Tribune* endorsed Nixon for reelection with this evaluation of his administration: "It has brought to virtual end the threat of ever increasing inflation at home."

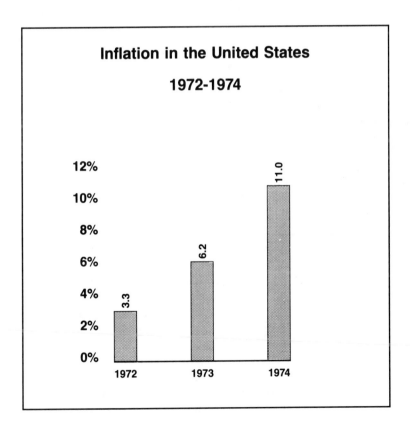

Inflation in the United States

1972-1974

Year	Inflation
1972	3.3
1973	6.2
1974	11.0

Wayne Owens

Congressman Wayne Owens in June 1972 foresaw a "good race" by Senator George McGovern in Utah. Owens said McGovern "will run well in Utah and has the potential of carrying the state against President Nixon."[20]

 Nixon carried Utah in 1972 with 324,000 votes to McGovern's 126,000.

Allen Howe

June 7, 1976

As a result of sex scandals which recently have rocked the House of Representatives, Congressman Allen Howe today urged strengthening of the House Ethics Committee. The Utah Democrat expressed deep concern about misconduct by congressmen which "casts a bad light on Congressional action as a whole."[21]

June 13, 1976

Two Salt Lake City Police officers, posing as prostitutes, arrested Representative Allen T. Howe late this evening for soliciting a sex act for hire after he had propositioned them.[22]

Orrin Hatch

In January 1976, before deciding to run for the U.S. Senate, Orrin Hatch sought the best advice he could find. Hatch turned to longtime friend Frank A. Madsen, Jr., now Hatch's chief counsel. Madsen, by virtue of his involvement in the Republican Party and his acquaintance with the Utah power structure, was in an excellent position to assist Hatch in making the correct decision. Madsen gave this counsel:

> I told him he was crazy even to consider such a run. I told him he didn't have a chance: He didn't know any of the state or community leaders; he had no money; he wasn't a member of the power structure; he had no political experience; he was not known in the

Republican Party; he had absolutely no name identification; very strong, well-known candidates had already announced their intention to file. There was just no possibility, I said.[23]

 Hatch defeated Senator Frank Moss in November.

Scott Matheson

Astrologer Sue Apitz predicted in January 1984 that Scott Matheson "will put all coyness aside and run for reelection." Apitz said the Matheson campaign "will flourish" in March.[24]

 On February 10, 1984, Matheson announced he would not seek reelection.

Two months later Matheson decided to try his luck at forecasting:

I have every confidence that Utahns will continue to support the policies which have served Utah well under Calvin Rampton and Scott Matheson by electing a Democratic governor.[25]

 Republican Bangerter won a lopsided victory.

Jake Garn

In January 1979, Jeanne Dixon, a nationally known crystal ball gazer, predicted Jake Garn would "have problems during the next few years and he won't run for the Senate in the next election."[26]

 Garn, who won reelection in 1980 by one of the widest margins in Utah history, is now seeking a third term.

Public Opinion Polls

An interesting phenomenon of most Utah public opinion polls is that when they turn out wrong, pollsters often state that "a highly volatile electorate" or "a sudden swing" in voter sentiment or a particular action by a candidate immediately before an election had a significant impact on the vote. When the polls are correct, however, we hear these assessments:

"On the button," "bullseye," "right on the nose," or "near perfect." (These comments have all been used by the *Salt Lake Tribune* to praise its Utah Poll.[27])

Following is a sampling of polls that weren't "on the button."

Dawson vs King, 1958

The *Tribune's* Utah Poll shows Representative William Dawson continuing to enjoy a good lead over Democratic challenger David S. King. With less than a week before the election, Dawson holds a 53.4 to 36.1 percent lead. Even if 100 percent of the undecided votes go to King, Dawson still would win by seven percent.[28]

 King won.

Creer vs Matheson, 1976

With the Democratic gubernatorial primary only one week away, the *Tribune's* Utah Poll shows John Preston Creer enjoying an impressive 45 to 32 percent lead over Scott Matheson. Creer's lead "was pervasive," noted the *Tribune,* "extending through every voter group."[29]

 Matheson crushed Creer, 51,000 to 35,000.

November 1980 elections

"When the dust died, the postelection autopsy showed that no Utah pollster had indicated a clear win for Jim Hansen over Gunn McKay, the extent of Bob Wright's support, or the sweep of Reagan's popularity," noted *Utah Holiday.*[30]

Wilson vs Hatch, 1982

"Recent polls in Utah show Hatch's race against Salt Lake Mayor Ted Wilson is closing...a KSL-TV poll on Thursday [October 28] had Hatch only three points ahead."[31]

 Five days later Hatch won by 58-41 percent.

Farley vs Monson, 1984

KUTV's early exit poll giving the Monson-Farley Second District Congressional race to Farley by 20 percentage points was dubbed "worst exit poll in history" by *Utah Holiday*. Even Mrs. Farley seemed persuaded by early results: "If he were a gentleman, he'd call me and concede right now."[32]

 Monson won by less than one percentage point.

Salt Lake Mayoral Election, 1985

Three days before the primary, mayoral candidate Jess Agraz reports that his own voter tracking "shows him leading the field, and he expects to be one of the two who survive." Agraz's campaign manager disputed reports that the final election would likely pit incumbent Mayor Palmer DePaulis against Merrill Cook: "Sure we're losing to Cook in Evanston and St. George. Who cares? He can be mayor there if he wants. But we're going to beat him in Salt Lake City."[33]

 On October 8, DePaulis captured 51 percent of the vote; Cook, 34 and Agraz 14.

NOTES FOR CHAPTER 4

1. *Salt Lake Tribune,* November 1, 1948, advertisement.
2. Dennis L. Lythgoe, *Let'em Holler,* 1982, p. 203.
3. *Deseret News,* June 28, 1956.
4. Ezra Taft Benson, *Cross Fire,* 1962, p. 70.
5. *New York Times,* September 16, 1953.
6. Ibid., September 17, 1953.
7. Benson, p. 220.
8. *New York Times,* February 21, 1958.
9. Ibid.
10. Benson, p. 405.
11. Ibid.
12. Ibid.
13. *Tribune,* November 4, 1958.
14. *Deseret News,* October 23, 1958.
15. Ibid., October 30, 1958.
16. *Tribune,* November 2, 1958.
17. Ibid., November 4, 1958.
18. Rampton to author, letter, December 17, 1985.
19. *Tribune,* February 13, 1964.
20. *Tribune,* June 14, 1972.
21. Ibid., June 8, 1976.
22. Ibid., June 14, 1976.
23. Madsen to author, letter, January 2, 1986.
24. *Utah Holiday,* January 1984.
25. *Tribune,* April 1, 1984.
26. *Utah Holiday,* August 1980.
27. *Tribune,* November 6, 1980, November 5, 1978, November 4, 1976.
28. Ibid., November 2, 1958.
29. Ibid., September 8, 1976.
30. *Utah Holiday,* January 1981.
31. *Deseret News,* October 29, 1982.
32. *Utah Holiday,* August 1985.
33. *Deseret News,* October 5, 1985.

Chapter 5

Addressing the Issues

Predicting Vietnam

Note: In 1973, the United States finally got out of South Vietnam, leaving the defense of that nation to those who, presumably, cared most about it — the South Vietnamese. Shortly thereafter, the North Vietnamese overran the country with ease.

"If we were to withdraw from Vietnam and turn that area over to our enemies, it would precipitate World War III."[1]

—Representative Laurence J. Burton
  February 18, 1966

"The picture in Viet Nam is a lot better than when we were here eight months ago."[2]

—Governor Calvin L. Rampton,
  following a briefing in
  Washington, D.C.,
  March 12, 1966

"The United States could be on the verge of a military breakthrough."

—Editorial,
  Salt Lake Tribune,
  April 23, 1966

During the mid-1960s, a group of Utahns supporting the Vietnam War staged a parade in downtown Salt Lake City. One of the placards read, "Surrender Viet Nam, California Next."[3]

"I agree fully with Gen. Westmoreland's stirring message to Congress."[4]

—Senator Wallace Bennett
July 21, 1967
(Westmoreland had told Congress: "We will prevail in Viet Nam over Communist aggression."[5])

"Am I an incurable pessimist? Far from it. I think we are winning this third world war, and at an increasingly rapid rate."[6]

—Senator Bennett
October 23, 1967

"We are in this war to win."[7]

—Ernest L. Wilkinson
(president, Brigham Young University),
May 18, 1968

"We never had the intention of really winning this war in the traditional sense — we only intended to effect a stalemate."[8]

—Ernest L. Wilkinson
May 29, 1970

"History will record [that Richard Nixon] had the courage to take decisive action to ensure that our goal of free choice for free nations is not destroyed by a last-gasp effort by a ruthless enemy."[9]

—Senator Bennett
April 24, 1972

The Equal Rights Amendment

Few issues in recent years have produced as much interest in Utah as the proposed Equal Rights Amendment. The LDS Church was accused of "a raw power play."[10] of "savage misogyny,"[11] and of being "the most ruthless opponent of women's rights."[12] One feminist columnist called ERA opponents "sexist rednecks" and "pea-brained brontosaurs, too inept to keep up with the tides of the future. '[13] The other side got in some licks, too. In December 1979, George Romney said ERA attracts "moral perverts" such as lesbians and homosexuals.[14]

Almost to the end, ERA supporters were willing to predict victory.

February 1975

By a 54-21 vote, the Utah House sent ERA down to another defeat. ERA supporters predicted that the defeat in Utah and in other states would have little ultimate effect, however, since only four more states were needed to ratify "and that total is expected to be gained with time to spare."[15]

November 1976

While many people were beginning to say the issue was dead, last Tuesday's elections prove otherwise, said Lynne Van Dam, president of the Utah Equal Rights coalition.[16]

October 1977

State Senator Frances Farley assured delegates of the Equal Rights Coalition that ERA will be ratified nationally.[17]

April 1978

In Salt Lake City, national feminist leader Bella Abzug predicted ERA will be ratified.[18]

August 1979

"We're dead serious about ERA, and it will be ratified," said Esther Landa, a member of President Carter's National Advisory Committee for Women. Mrs. Landa noted that recent rejection of ERA by the Utah legislature "made Utah the laughing stock of the nation."[19]

December 1979

Feminist author and ex-Mormon Marilyn Warenski predicted on December 9 that the Mormon Church's excommunication of Sonia Johnson will be a tremendous boost for the ERA.[20]

June 1981

There has been an "upsurge of interest" in ERA in Utah, said Barbara Hutchinson, director of the Women's Department of the American Federation of Government Employees. Ms. Hutchinson noted that only three more states are needed to ratify ERA, and Utah could be one of them.[21]

 ERA died in June 1982 three states short of ratification.

Fiction: During the struggle surrounding the proposed ERA, opponents sometimes claimed Utah was the first state or territory to give women the right to vote. Even the *Los Angeles Times* picked up on this assertion: "Utah women were the first women in the nation given the right to vote in a national election."[22]

Fact: Wyoming, on December 10, 1869, extended suffrage to women, edging out Utah by two months.

The MX Missile System

"We have the support of the Mormon Church."[23]

—Air Force general,
  commenting on MX in a
  southern Utah town meeting,
  1981

"There's nothing you can do about it, Frances. The governor has invited it into Utah, and the President is going to announce his support for the project within a few weeks."[24]

—Committee Chairman,
  MX bearings,
  August 1979

 Frances Farley spearheaded the successful fight against locating MX in Utah.

Do Reasonable People Oppose MX?

"Reasonable people would have to conclude we've got to have the MX," said Senator Orrin Hatch on July 18, 1980.[25]

Congressman Dan Marriott also had a low opinion of unreasonable people who would oppose MX: "[They are] people with their heads in the sand."[26]

 In May 1981, the First Presidency of the Mormon Church announced the Church's opposition to locating MX in Utah.

MX myth: As a result of the Mormon Church's opposition to MX in Utah, public opinion in the state turned against the project.

Fact: Utah already opposed MX. One 1980 survey showed Utahns about 2-1 against MX.[27] Another survey, conducted by Wasatch Opinion Research in February 1981, showed 52 percent of Wasatch Front residents opposed the project and 53 percent in southwestern Utah opposed it. [28] Following the LDS statement, however, polls did indicate an increase in opposition to the project.[29]

Completing the Interstate

June 1986 marked the 30th anniversary of a measure passed by Congress authorizing construction of the U.S. interstate highway system. Of the 42,500 mile interstate, Utah was targeted for 938 miles.

According to the 1956 bill, the system was to have been completed by 1972.

 In May 1986, Utah Department of Transportation spokesmen said only 815 miles had been finished in Utah. UDOT is hopeful that the remaining 123 miles will be ready by 1992.

On June 5, 1978, engineers in charge of I-215 Belt Route planning predicted all construction would be completed by November 1984.[30]

 On January 22, 1986, the project engineer gave these revised completion dates:[31]

> I-215 for I-80 to 2200 North: Fall 1986
> I-215 and California Ave. Interchange: Spring 1987
> I-215 from 2100 So. to I-80: Fall 1988
> I-215 from 100 E. to 20th East: Fall 1987
> I-215 from 20th E. to 4500 South: Fall 1989

Naturally, say engineers, these dates are contingent upon funds being allocated by Congress.

CUP Runneth Over

July 17, 1956

Utah Congressman William Dawson today observed that the overall price of the entire Central Utah Project will be $208 million.[32]

Representative Henry Dixon of Utah says the project will not add to the current agricultural surpluses because "it is estimated that by 1975 every acre of tillable land will be required to provide the food and fiber needs of the United States." In the coming years our food surpluses "will have long ceased to exist,"[33] said Dixon.

 The exact opposite has occurred. Record productivity has kept prices paid agricultural producers low, thereby allowing fewer farmers than ever before to meet the food and fiber needs of the United States.

October 12, 1965

According to a news report prepared by the Central Utah Water Conservancy District, the Bonneville Unit of the Central Utah Project could be completed as soon as 1980 and as late as 1985. Cost will be $323.8 million.[34]

July 18, 1968

Senator Wallace Bennett today observed that the Bureau of Reclamation "has indicated delivery of Colorado River water to Salt Lake County and part of Utah County can be a reality as early as 1972."[35]

Initial CUP water arrived in Salt Lake County in May 1986.

August 21, 1980

Lynn S. Ludlow, manager of the Central Utah Water Conservancy District, says the Bonneville Unit of the Central Utah project will cost about $1 billion rather than the nearly $325 million estimated in 1965.[36]

November 1985

On November 19, Utah voters approved repayment of an extra $335 million to continue work on the Bonneville Unit of the Central Utah Project. The estimated cost of the Bonneville Unit is now $2.2 billion. Supporters say "critical shortages" of water will occur by 1995 without the project. [37]

Going for the Gold

The 1972 Winter Olympics

Early in 1966, Salt Lake City was selected as the United States nominee to host the 1972 Winter Olympics. All that remained was for Salt Lake City to convince the International Olympic Committee (IOC).

"Utah fully expects to obtain the winter games in 1972."[38]

—Max E. Rich
(president of the Olympics for Utah, Inc.),
January 25, 1966

"The 1972 Winter Olympics in Utah will be the greatest ever."[39]

—Senator Frank Moss
March 14, 1966

"[Salt Lake City's Olympic claims] are far more formidable and creditable than those advanced by Banff and Sapporo — which also have put their best feet forward in their presentation volumes."

—*Salt Lake Tribune*
March 27, 1966

"We don't believe it. We bet IOC will vote 60 per cent for Utah after a preliminary round in which Lahti, Finland; and Sapporo, Japan, are eliminated."

—Robert Woody
*(*Tribune *business writer),*
responding to claims that
Canada would be selected,
March 29, 1966

"It will be delightful, and we certainly urge you to participate with us in

1972 when the Olympics come to Utah."[40]

—Representative Laurence Burton,
   addressing Congress,
   April 4, 1966

"Our chances are excellent."[41]

—Max E. Rich,
   April 18, 1966

"Salt Lake City officials are enthusiastic about their chances."

—*Salt Lake Tribune,*
   April 20, 1966

"I think our chances of winning this competition are excellent."[42]

—Max E. Rich,
   April 20, 1966

"[Utah is] highly confident it will gain the nod to stage the 1972 Winter Games."

—*Salt Lake Tribune*
   April 23, 1966

 On April 26, Sapporo, Japan, was awarded the 1972 Winter Olympic Games. An International Olympics Committee source revealed that Sapporo received 32 votes to 16 for runnerup Canada. Salt Lake City, with four votes, finished last in the balloting.

The 1976 Winter Olympics

Salt Lake City Commissioner James L. Barker, Jr., said on April 26, 1966, that he feels certain the Winter Olympics will come to Utah in 1976. Marvin C. Jenson, a Salt Lake County commissioner, declared that "Utah will be far better prepared to offer a bid for 1976."[43]

 Utah did not bid on the 1976 games.

The 1992 Olympics

In 1985, Salt Lake City again made an Olympics bid, this time for the 1992 winter games. First step of the process was to earn the selection of the United States Olympic Committee (USOC).

"Next time the flame stops here."[44]

—Mayor Ted Wilson,
  after running the Los Angeles
  Summer Olympics torch up State
  Street to Capitol Hill,
  1984

"Reno-Lake Tahoe and Salt Lake City are the front runners to gain USOC support for 1992."

—*Deseret News*
  March 12, 1985

"Salt Lake City has a better than 50-50 chance of being selected the U.S. representative to host the 1992 Winter Olympics, according to an 800-page report detailing the feasibility of a Wasatch Front Olympics."

—*Deseret News*
  May 2, 1985

"We feel that we will get the USOC sanction to seek the international bid."[45]

—Tom Welch
  (chairman of the Salt Lake
  Winter Games Organizing Committee),
  May 2, 1985

"But every indication I have, and I believe it's based on rational thinking, is that Salt Lake will get the U.S. bid."[46]

—Tom Welch
  May 30, 1985

"If we lose the bid — *which we won't* — it would be like raising funds for a losing candidate after an election is over. It would be very difficult."[47]

—Mayor Wilson,
  encouraging stepped-up
  fundraising efforts,
  May 30, 1985

"[Olympic proponents] don't see how they can lose."

—*Deseret News,*
   June 13, 1985

 Salt Lake City's $500,000 effort fell short. On June 16, USOC selected Anchorage as its nominee to host the 1992 games. Lake Placid finished second in the balloting. Early reports had said "a stunned S.L. comes in 2nd." Not true, said USOC official Mike Moran: "Salt Lake was not within shooting distance of gaining the nod."[48]

Olympics Fever Burns Again

Although Salt Lake City failed to win the 1992 Winter Olympics, "chances are looking better and better that Salt Lake County could be awarded the 1990 International Law Enforcement Olympics," said Mike Julian, president of the Utah Law Enforcement Olympics Federation. "We hope to know Friday whether we'll host the games or not. It's looking good at this point."[49] (February 19, 1986)

On February 21, 1986, Edmonton, Canada, was awarded the 1990 International Law Enforcement Olympics.

NOTES FOR CHAPTER 5
1. *Salt Lake Tribune,* February 19, 1966.
2. Ibid., March 13, 1966.
3. Ibid., October 17, 1965.
4. Wallace Bennett newsletter, Congressional Record, July 21, 1967, p. 19701.
5. Ibid.
6. Congressional Record, October 23, 1967, p. 29689.
7. Ernest L. Wilkinson, *Earnestly Yours,* 1971, p. 82.
8. Ibid., p. 83.
9. *Tribune,* April 25, 1972.
10. *Phoenix Gazette,* February 20, 1975.
11. Sonia Johnson.
12. Byron Marchant, member of Quorum of Twelve Apostates, letter to *Salt Lake Tribune,* March 4, 1981.
13. Joan Beck, columnist, *Chicago Tribune.*
14. *Salt Lake Tribune,* December 19, 1979.
15. *Atlanta Constitution,* February 18, 1975, editorial.
16. *Tribune,* November 9, 1976.
17. Ibid., October 28, 1977.
18. Ibid., April 27, 1978.
19. Ibid., August 26, 1979.
20. Ibid., December 9, 1979.
21. Ibid., June 16, 1981.
22. *Los Angeles Times,* June 26, 1983.
23. *Utah Holiday,* August 1981.
24. Farley to author, letter, December 14, 1985.
25. *Tribune,* June 19, 1980.
26. Ibid., October 24, 1979.
27. The MX Missile System, Oversight Hearings, Serial No. 96-30, 1980.
28. *Deseret News,* May 25, 1981.
29. Ibid.
30. *Tribune,* June 6, 1978.
31. Sheldon W. McConkie, District 2 director, Utah State Department of Transportation, letter to author, January 22, 1986.
32. Congressional Record, July 17, 1956, p. 13217.
33. Ibid., February 7, 1956, p. 2268. See also Congressional Record, July 17, 1956, Dixon.
34. Ibid., October 12, 1965, p. 26665.
35. Ibid., July 18, 1968, p. 21982.
36. *Tribune,* August 21, 1980.
37. Central Utah Water Conservancy District, brochure, November 1985.
38. *Tribune,* January 26, 1986.
39. Congressional Record, March 14, 1966, p. 5593.
40. Ibid., April 4, 1966, p. 7511.
41. *Tribune,* April 19, 1966.
42. Ibid., April 21, 1966.
43. Ibid., April 27, 1966.
44. *Utah Holiday,* June 1985.
45. *Deseret News,* May 3, 1985.
46. Ibid., May 30, 1985.
47. Ibid.
48. *Tribune,* June 21, 1985.
49. *Deseret News,* February 20, 1986.

Chapter 6

Salt Lake City Government

Battling the Bats

August 1973

Bats in the City and County Building "were exterminated several months ago," according to Leonard Cosco, assistant to City Commissioner Conrad Harrison.[1]

February 1975

Bats, which recently appeared in the fourth floor offices of the city's Building and Housing Services, have finally been driven from the City and County Building, say city officials. Supervisors used a long-handled "bat catcher" to solve the problem. As an additional guarantee against future bat problems, a carpenter screened outside openings to windows.[2]

August 1976

Bats have again been seen flying through the city's Building and Housing Services Department. "We're trying to plug up the holes before they return," said Commissioner Jess Agraz.[3]

December 1976

A recurring bat problem has driven city officials to using ultrasonic sound to drive the bats out. Three new machines creating high level noises should interfere with the bats' inborn "radar" and keep them away, predicted John Hiskey, assistant Parks Superintendent.[4]

March 1977

A battery of experts agreed the bats have left the City and County Building. "I think they're gone," said Craig E. Peterson, Building and Housing director. "The noise machines ran all night and we haven't heard a squeak today."[5]

1979

Building and Housing Services employees report that bats have again been spotted on several occasions this year in their offices.[6]

1984

"BHS employees are at their wits end in attempting to get rid of the bats," said city building inspector Bill Cupit.

Some employees, said Cupit, have tried a few "home" remedies to get rid of the pests. One employee poured Clorox inside the walls, but succeeded only in bleaching his shoes. Another poured ammonia into the walls. This woke all the bats and made them squeaking mad.

Building and Housing employees recently presented Mayor Wilson with a petition pleading for help in eliminating bats in the City and County Building. In response, a professional exterminator was called in and "the bats now have taken flight."[7]

Elusive Renovation Costs

Predicting the costs of both building the City and County Building and renovating it have proved elusive. The structure was to have been built at a cost of $350,000, but ended up costing $900,000. Projecting renovation costs has been even more difficult.

The building's restoration project was initiated in 1973 at a then estimated cost of *$3.2 million.*[8]

On September 5, 1976, the city engineer in charge of restoration projected the final bill near *$10 million.*[9]

Cost of restoring the building's sagging sandstone in March 1982 was put at *$18.1 million* by Donald Spencer, Salt Lake County's Public Works director.[10]

Estimates range from *$13 to $25 million* to complete various renovation options, said city administrator Phil Erickson in the August 1982 issue of the *Official Rumor,* a Salt Lake City employee publication.

On September 14, 1983, the draft report of a $206,000 study on restoration projected a *$21.5 million* price tag.[11]

On November 20, 1983, final costs projected by the Gustavson-Ehrenkrantz study places the bill at *$30.3 million.*[12]

Salt Lake City voters on April 29, 1986, approved general obligation bonds to renovate the City and County Building. Maximum amount of bonds that can be sold will be *$34.5 million.*[13]

City financial experts on May 14, 1986, were pleased to report that debt service for the general obligation bonds will run only $3 million annually instead of the $3.5 to $4 million originally thought.[14] Total principal and interest costs over the 25-year payback will be about *$80 million.*

Note: The more recent renovation estimates include costs of new electrical, cooling, and plumbing systems. Naturally, none of the preceding estimates include the several million dollars already spent on exterior restoration.

"Keep Your Money," Says Mayor

January 6, 1976

Mayor Ted Wilson said he promised during his campaign not to accept a pay raise unless it is a cost-of-living hike. "I plan to stick to that promise and I won't take this raise if it's approved," the mayor told fellow comissioners in today's discussion of city pay raises.[15]

January 21, 1976

"I'll only take the cost of living part of the raise," pledged Mayor Wilson today. "People run for office not for salaries."[16]

 In the summer of 1979, mayoral candidate Doug Bowers pointed out that Mayor Wilson had taken five pay raises in three years.

"It's a position I changed my mind on." responded Wilson. "I'm worth every dime I get."[17]

Officials too Career Oriented, says Mayor

January 2, 1979

Salt Lake City Mayor Ted Wilson announced today that he would not seek reelection as mayor of Salt Lake City. Wilson observed that "elected officials are often too career oriented. Our system would be better if we alternated public and private life a little more."[18]

June 7, 1979

Mayor Wilson announced today he would seek reelection after all because "the city needs experienced leadership for the transition [to Mayor-Council]."[19]

January 21, 1982

Mayor Wilson announced today his candidacy for the U.S. Senate.[20]

September 13, 1983

Mayor Wilson today kicked off his campaign for third term as mayor of Salt Lake City. "It seems like I'm always running for something," he noted.[21]

October 24, 1983

Mayor Wilson told newsmen today he has no plans on running for any state or national office in 1984, but he did not know what his plans would be later.[22]

Surplus? What Surplus?

January 17, 1980

City budget officials say this year's revenue surplus will be nowhere near the $3.1 million reached last fiscal year.

"My private estimate is that it will be about $500,000," said J. Alan Blodgett, the city's temporary budget director.

"I don't know if we will have a tax surplus this year," said Mayor Wilson. It's both "too early" and "bad timing," said the mayor, to talk of a surplus at a time when Salt Lake City is trying to persuade the state legislature not to reduce utility franchise taxes from eight percent to four percent.[23]

On February 19, 1980, Salt Lake City came up with a $7.4 million budget surplus, the largest in history. It included $700,000 that had been "found" only a week earlier.[24]

They're Guilty!

News media are frequently criticized for using the appellation, "suspects," for those accused of crimes, particularly when the public is convinced the "suspects" are guilty. Although those who appear to be plainly guilty are usually convicted, it is the exception that makes the rule.

In a November 26, 1976, editorial, "Fire the Lot," the *Salt Lake Tribune* forgot to extend the presumption of innocence to several Salt Lake City policemen, and made the following comments on a matter still under investigation:

> Some Salt Lake City Police Department employees who allege they are motorcycle officers aren't fit to be issued kiddy cars. They are the individuals, all pouty and petulant because they will no longer be allowed to play games with taxpayer money, who deliberately damaged 10 police motorcycles.
>
> Their infantile behavior was in apparent retaliation for department decisions to disband the motorcycle squad; a long time questionable use of law enforcement dollars...
>
> Their vandalism sullies the memory of those officers who have given their lives in the line of duty.
>
> The malicious damaging of public property demands immediate and irrevocable dismissal, along with criminal prosecution of those responsible...
>
> If these underdeveloped men can't be trusted to take proper care of public property, it is a certainty they are so gravely immature they should not be allowed loose in the community with a gun hanging from their hip.

 The investigation, completed within a week, exonerated the officers of all charges.

Swift Justice

Salt Lake City Police Chief Bud Willoughby assured reporters on October 15, 1985, that enough "incriminating evidence" had been found in the car of bombing suspect Mark Hofmann to permit the filing of charges October 16th relating to three separate bombing incidents in Salt Lake City.

"We've found enough evidence that [federal agent] Gary Miller is going to the U.S. Attorney's Office to file charges. Gary feels in his gut that we have more than enough [to charge Mr. Hofmann]," the chief said.[25]

 Charges were filed against Hofmann on February 4, 1986.

NOTES FOR CHAPTER 6

1. *Salt Lake Tribune,* August 3, 1973.
2. Ibid., February 13, 1975.
3. Ibid., August 31, 1976.
4. Ibid., December 13, 1976.
5. Ibid., March 26, 1977.
6. Fourth floor Building and Housing employees to author, a fifth-floor Building and Housing employee in 1979.
7. *Official Rumor,* Salt Lake City employee newspaper, 1984.
8. *Tribune,* February 25, 1982. (Refers to 1973 estimate.)
9. Ibid., September 5, 1976.
10. Ibid., March 2, 1982.
11. Gustavson-Ehrenkrantz study, draft report.
12. Ibid., final report.
13. *Deseret News,* March 5, 1986.
14. Ibid., May 14, 1986.
15. Ibid., January 7, 1976.
16. *Tribune,* January 22, 1976.
17. *Utah Holiday,* August 1979.
18. *Tribune,* January 3, 1979.
19. Ibid., June 8, 1979.
20. Ibid., January 22, 1982.
21. Ibid., September 14, 1983.
22. *Deseret News,* October 25, 1983.
23. *Tribune,* January 18, 1980.
24. Ibid., February 20, 1980.
25. Ibid., October 16, 1985.

Part 3

Utah Features

Chapter 7

Mother Nature

Early Weather Assessments

"These valleys are lofty, narrow, and parched by intense drouth from May to November."[1]

—Horace Greeley
(editor of the New York Tribune),
1859

"[Jim Bridger] passed through that country a year ago last summer in the month of July [1845], and they generally had one or two showers every day."[2]

—in *Founding of an Empire*

"Utah has no earthquakes, no tornadoes, cyclones, blizzards, or sandstorms. There is no rainy season, no drizzling rains, cold damps or fierce winds, no cases of sunstroke, malaria here finds no lurking place, and dew is seldom seen."

—*Salt Lake Tribune*
December 8, 1896

Long-term Forecasts

How accurate are long-term forecasts of Utah weather?

In 1979, KUTV meteorologist Mark Eubank did an analysis of the National Weather Service's thirty-day forecasts for 1975-1978. His study produced this remarkable result:

> A more accurate and skillful forecast of Utah's temperatures and precipitation could have been made during the past four years by predicting the exact opposite of the government's 30-day forecasts![3]

Short-term Forecasts

With weather forecasters expected to make 365 predictions yearly, even a 90-percent accuracy rate would soon yield enough bad predictions to fill a volume. Only one example, therefore, of a less-than-accurate short-term forecast is included:

October 16, 1984 (Tuesday)

"Chance of showers decreasing some Thursday."

—National Weather Service

October 17, 1984 (Wednesday)

"Mostly cloudy with decreasing snow showers through Thursday."

—National Weather Service

October 18, 1984 (Thursday)

"Salt Lake and Davis counties were paralyzed Thursday morning by the worst snowstorm ever recorded since Salt Lake Airport started keeping records in 1928."

—*Deseret News*

Windproof?

On September 21, 1952, KSL-TV announced construction of a 370-foot transmitting tower to be built on Coon Peak which went into operation on November 15. The tower, engineered to withstand high wind speeds, was the highest TV transmitter in the world.[4]

 On December 5, 1952, high winds toppled KSL's new transmitting tower on Coon Peak. No difficulty was reported at KDYL's tower 3.5 miles away.[5]

WIND RELATED?
YES I CAN CONFIRM
THAT OUR VIDEO PROBLEMS
ARE WIND RELATED.

No Floods This Spring?

March 25, 1953

Although the city experienced some of its worst flooding in history in 1952, C. W. Wilson, Salt Lake's Water Department superintendent, assured city residents that there will be no floods to contend with this spring.[6]

April 7, 1953

Under the headline, "Recall '52 Floods? We're Ready Now," the *Salt Lake Tribune* reported that Salt Lake City officials feel the city is nearly certain to avoid flooding this spring. New engineering works were cited as the reason.[7]

April 17, 1953

Heavy flooding in Salt Lake City has turned the area from 900 South to 1300 South Main Street into a "new lagoon" say angry merchants in the area. The merchants pointed out that 1.42 inches of rain were needed in April 1952 to flood the same area that today was flooded with only .96 inches. The merchants were especially bitter over promises by city spokesmen a month ago claiming measures of the past year would forestall new flooding.[8]

April 18, 1980

Terry Holzworth, director of Salt Lake County Flood Control, said there is little chance of a repeat of the 1952 flood ever occurring again in Salt Lake. Holzworth pointed out that storm drains have been increased and improved, and the surplus canal would carry much more water.[9]

September 30, 1982

Following record rains of last week, Salt Lake County has installed new flood control policies and procedures. Officials are convinced these measures will reduce future flooding problems.[10]

Photos show the 13th South river in the 1952 flood (top) and in 1983.

February 9, 1983

"There is no indication at this time that flooding will occur," said John Patton, hydrologist for the National Weather Service, when asked about the possibility of spring flooding in Salt Lake City. The weather service "is predicting a good runoff season throughout the state," Patton said.[11]

 Salt Lake City experienced the worst flooding in its history during the late spring of 1983.

Earthquakes

Many predictions of earthquakes cannot easily be proved inaccurate because they refer only to probabilities of quakes occurring within certain time periods in the distant future. Occasionally, however, someone comes along who is willing to go out on the limb with a forecast.

In 1963, ecclesiastical writer Norman C. Pierce envisioned "the greatest earthquake in history" hitting Utah: "Watch for it late in 1967!"[12]

Early in 1983, a fundamentalist preacher from southern Utah predicted an earth upheaval that would swallow up Salt Lake City in November of that year.[13]

An astrologer appearing on KSL-TV's "Prime Time Access" in early January 1985 predicted a major Utah quake for January 17, 1985.[14]

Conference Weather — Myth or Reality?

Certainly it doesn't always rain on LDS general conference weekend, as some have claimed over the years. Yet weather data for the past 98 years indicate that claims of unusually wet weather at conference time are essentially accurate, especially during April conferences, which are rained on almost 70 percent of the time.[15] A study of rainfall totals on weekends before general conference, after conference, and on conference weekends, shows that for the period analyzed, 1957-1981, conference weekend totals exceeded both pre- and post-conference weekends by a significant amount.[16]

Utah's "Dependable" Snow

On March 14, 1966, Senator Frank Moss assured Congress that Utah was a great site for the 1972 Winter Olympics because "we have the finest powder snow in the world, *dependable in depth throughout a 6-month ski season.*"[17]

Remember the winter of 1976-77?

November 15, 1976

Although ski resorts are short of snow so far, "skiers are going to get in so many ski days a season — no matter what," said Craig Badami, marketing director for Park City Ski Corporation.[18]

December 4, 1976

A weather forecasting technique called "Lag Effects in Weather Predictions" is being refined at BYU. "North Utah ski interests will be pleased to know...that total snowfall for December could exceed 20 inches at some ski resorts — particularly Alta," say the BYU educators in charge of the computerized prediction project.[19]

December 9, 1976

Snowless ski slopes have forced resort managers at Alta, Snowbird and Park City to lay off more than 1,000 employees. At Alta things are so slow that remaining employees are painting everything capable of holding paint.[20]

December 18, 1976

" 'The Greatest Snow on Earth' is somewhere else this year — in New England, in the Himalayas, in the Arctic," said one news report. Alta Mayor William Levitt figures the loss to Alta and its lodges is already about $1.3 million. The resorts are featuring snowless events.[21]

January 27, 1977

Snowmaking equipment is now being installed at Park City. Lack of snow has cancelled most local ski competitions.[22]

 In the 1976-77 winter, Utah's ski industry lost $25 million. Meanwhile, eastern resorts generally reported record years.[23]

NOTES FOR CHAPTER 7

1. Leland Hargrave Creer, *Founding of an Empire,* 1947, p. 417.
2. Ibid., p. 288.
3. Mark Eubank, *Utah Weather,* 1979, p. 55.
4. *Deseret News,* September 21, 1952.
5. Ibid., December 6, 1952.
6. *Salt Lake Tribune,* March 26, 1953.
7. Ibid., April 8, 1953.
8. Ibid., April 18, 1953.
9. Ibid., April 19, 1980.
10. Ibid., September 30, 1982, editorial.
11. Ibid., February 10, 1983.
12. Norman C. Pierce, *The 3½ Years,* 1963.
13. Recollected by Sam Weller, Zion's Book-Store, note to author.
14. "Prime Time Access," KSL-TV, January 2, 1986 (This program featured a review of predictions made in a January 1985 show).
15. *Deseret News,* April 4, 1986.
16. Ibid., March 31, 1982.
17. Congressional Record, March 14, 1966, p. 5593.
18. *Tribune,* November 16, 1976.
19. Ibid., December 5, 1976.
20. Ibid., December 10, 1976.
21. Ibid., December 19, 1976.
22. Ibid., January 28, 1977.
23. Ibid., May 1, 1977.

Chapter 8

Sports

It is impossible to consider even a fraction of Utah sporting miscalculations. This section is necessarily limited to a brief look at a few, mostly recent highlights.

The Utah Jazz

"The train only comes by once, and I just don't think Salt Lake is a big enough market to handle what it would cost to get in [the NBA]."[1]

—Bill Daniels
(former owner of the Utah Stars),
December 1, 1975

"Nissalke...is more than a mere coach — he's the franchise. Without Nissalke the chances of the Jazz ever rearing its beaten brow from the cellar of the division are slim indeed."[2]

—Richard Barnum-Reece
(Utah sportswriter),
1981

 Under Coach Frank Layden, the Jazz have compiled the best records in franchise history and have qualified for the NBA playoffs three years in a row.

"[The franchise is] in the best position it's ever been...[I now have] the most confidence I've ever had about the future success of the franchise."[3]

—Sam Battistone
(Jazz owner),
May 26, 1983

"Battistone's team is $6 million to $7 million in debt and the financial wolves have been baying at the door for the six years the team has been in Utah...for all the good intentions, the debt still remains."

—*Deseret News*
March 22, 1985

(Note: In April 1985, when car dealer Larry H. Miller bought half of the team for $8 million, the Jazz again were said to be on solid footing. But on June 13, 1986, the Jazz were nearly sold to a Minnesota group. Only Miller's 11th-hour decision to buy 100 percent of the team kept the franchise in Utah.)

1983-84 Jazz

"[The Jazz] have been everybody's pick to return to the basement after a year of subletting it to Houston."

—Lex Hemphill
*(*Salt Lake Tribune *sportswriter),*
October 26, 1983

The Jazz will finish 24-58 in 1983-84.

—*Basketball Digest*
November 1983

"Utah will have a tough time not slipping behind the up-and-coming Rockets into last place in the division."

—*The 1984 Complete Handbook of Pro Basketball*

"The season could be over before it begins."[4]

—Dave Blackwell
(Utah sportswriter),
on the prospect of playing several
early road games in Las Vegas

 In the 1983-84 season, the Jazz finished with a 45-37 record, the best in franchise history, and claimed first place in the Western Division.

Spirits in the Palace

After the demise of the Utah Stars in 1975, the American Basketball Association in May 1976 approved the move of the Spirits of St. Louis franchise to Salt Lake City. On May 20, the *Salt Lake Tribune* ran this headline: "There'll be 'Spirits' in Salt Palace This Winter." So excited was Spirits' President Harry Weltman about the move to Salt Lake City, that he said:

> We are basically here to stay. We came here only after a careful study of the Salt Lake market potential. We hope to keep the franchise here forever.[5]

 Less than a month later, the American Basketball Association folded up. Not a single game was played by the Utah Spirits.

Golden Eagles

"[The Golden Eagles are] the best minor league hockey franchise in the solar system. Bar none. Without exception.

"When you talk about premier this and premier that, save a place for the Eagles. The are the class of their league — or any minor hockey league. In their world they are the rulers, the monarchs. They not only sit on the king's throne, they own it."

—Craig Haslam
(editor, Spectrum),
January 27, 1982

"It should be a great decade for Golden Eagles hockey fans in the Mountain West."[6]

—*Mountainwest* magazine
   1981

On May 21, 1984, the Central Hockey League folded up after 21 years of play, leaving the Golden Eagles leagueless. The Eagles later joined the International Hockey League, but attendance has declined from about 7,500 per game to 3,500.[7] Despite the deteriorating financial picture, owner Art Teece, battling and determined, is taking steps to keep the team in Salt Lake City.

Incidentally, *Mountainwest,* which predicted "a great decade" for the Eagles, also commented on the magazine's own future in its September-October 1981 issue: "We at *Mountainwest* are proud of our past and pleased with the prospects for our future." The magazine went out of business a year later.

Salt Lake Trappers

If any professional franchise in recent Utah sports memory had the prospect of doing poorly, it was the 1985 Salt Lake Trappers, an independent entry into baseball's Pioneer League. The reason? The entire team consisted exclusively of cast-offs, players who had been rejected by the major league scouts. They would be competing against teams made up of players under contract to major league teams. Undaunted, the Trappers proceeded to capture the southern division championship. On September 4, playing on the home field of the favored Great Falls Dodgers, winners of the northern division, the Trappers upended the Dodgers, 8-6, to win the league championship. No wonder pitcher Ed McCarter, the day after Salt Lake's big win, said: "I don't think the scouts are doing a very good job."[8]

Major league teams have since repented, drafting nine members of the 1985 Trappers.

A before and after assessment of key players:[9]

Chuck Heist

Considered a poor prospect by major league scouts. Played poorly earlier in the 1985 season at Idaho Falls, but was picked up in mid-season by the Trappers. Heist proceeded to hit .322, finished seventh in the league in RBIs, and drove in four runs in the championship game. Coach Jim Gattis later described the trade which brought Heist to Salt Lake as "the Heist heist."

Scott Melvin

"Not a big league prospect," said scouts before the season. Melvin led all second basemen in fielding and finished third in the league with a .351 batting average.

Mark Grimes

Considered too slow by scouts who timed him at 7.2 for 60 yards, apparently using a cheap watch. The Trappers timed him at 6.8. Grimes hit .342 and finished with 55 RBIs, second in the league.

Jay Slotnick

Not drafted by the pros due to lack of upper body strength. All-star Slotnick hit .324 and had 53 RBIs, tied for third in the league. Slotnik proved strong enough to tie teammate Chuck Heist with 11 triples, a league record.

Ed McCarter

McCarter was rejected by the scouts because he didn't throw hard enough. But he led the league with 111 strikeouts and in complete games with eight. A league all-star, McCarter has been the winning pitcher in the last two league championship games. (In 1984, he was with Helena.)

WAC Football Dominance

"I don't see any big shots emerging like USC and UCLA in the PAC-10... the league will be more balanced...And let's face it, in this area there is not really great football support...Places like BYU and Utah should have stadiums of 60 thousand seating, but they don't for lack of support."[10]

—John Mooney
(Tribune *sports editor*),
September 1977

BYU has won outright or shared the WAC football championship ten consecutive years. Although many in Provo had decried expansion of Cougar Stadium to 65,000 seats, anticipating high vacancy rates, games are consistently sold out.

NOTES FOR CHAPTER 8

1. *Salt Lake Tribune,* December 2, 1975.
2. *Utah Holiday,* January 1981.
3. *Tribune,* May 26, 1983.
4. *Utah Holiday,* December, 1983.
5. *Tribune,* May 20, 1976.
6. *Mountainwest,* Vol. 7 #1, 1981.
7. *Deseret News,* February 2, 1986.
8. Ed McCarter to Salt Lake City TV newsman, September 5, 1985.
9. Based on 1986 author interview with Van Schley, Trapper player personnel supplier.
10. *Mountainwest,* September 1977.

Chapter 9

Short Subjects

The Mormon Will

The difficulty of authenticating documents, highlighted by the Mark Hofmann bomb trial in Salt Lake City, is nothing new to Utahns.

In 1976, a handwritten will attributed to billionaire Howard Hughes turned up in Mormon Church headquarters. Delivery of the will was eventually traced to Melvin Dummar, a Utah gas station operator who, coincidentally, was left one-sixteenth of the Hughes empire in the will. Controversy over the "Mormon will" raged for two years.

"I am sure the document was written by Mr. Hughes and the signature is indeed genuine. The signatures look exactly like Hughes."[1]

—Charles Hamilton
  (New York City handwriting expert),
  April 30, 1976

"[The will] could not be a forgery."[2]

—Noah Dietrich
  (executor of the will),
  May 4, 1976

"It is not in the realm of possibility [for Dummar to have forged the will]."[3]

—Harold Rhoden
  (attorney to Noah Dietrich),
  May 4, 1976

"I think the will is real."[4]

—Bonnie Dummar
  (wife of Melvin Dummar),
  January 13, 1977

"[Forensic tests give] one of the strongest physical indications we have that the will was written by Hughes...we don't have a fingerprint, or a movie of his writing it, but we've got about the next best thing."[5]

—Harold Rhoden
  September 8, 1977

"I am convinced that the will was written by Howard R. Hughes."[6]

—Arnold Etman
  (former Ministry of Justice hand-
  writing expert from Holland),
  December 15, 1977

"In my soul and conscience, I can say that this document is authentic."[7]

—Pierre Faideau
  (forensic handwriting expert from Paris),
  January 9, 1978

"Howard Hughes — that's certain,"[8]

—Dr. Henri Ollivier
  (director of the police laboratory
  in Marseilles, France),
  responding to the question: Who wrote the will?,
  March 9, 1978

On June 8, 1978, a Nevada jury found the Howard Hughes will to be a fraud. On December 5, 1978, superior court Judge Jack Swink of Los Angeles ruled after one hour of testimony "without any question the will is invalid...a forgery and a fake."[9]

Geneva's Bright Future

The following quotations about Geneva Steel are Utah newspaper headlines and article excerpts forecasting a bright future for the firm.

March 8, 1966

"Geneva Vows To Win Survival Fight"

—*Deseret News*

May 4, 1967

"Geneva Plant Future Assured, U.S. Steel Chief Assures Utah"

—*Salt Lake Tribune*

September 8, 1973

"Geneva Steel dying? Couldn't be healthier" "U.S. Steel is too smart to put money into a mill that it's going to shut down," said Geneva superintendent Raymond W. Sundquist.

—*Deseret News*

February 3, 1974

"Geneva Steel Firm 'Alive,' Healthy"

—*Salt Lake Tribune*

June 14, 1980

"Executive Optimistic on Geneva Works"

—*Salt Lake Tribune*

Fall 1985

"The reports of our death are highly exaggerated."

—*Geneva Bulletin*

(In the fall 1985 bulletin, "Out to Win in the West," Geneva's general manager emphasized that the key to Geneva's future is productivity. He quoted a *Provo Herald* editorial of July 1984: "The key to Geneva's survival is production and profitability...If Geneva makes money — and lately it has been — it will survive." The bulletin praised Geneva's workers for making operations profitable in 1985, citing all-time productivity records set in 1985 including most steel produced in one month at the 45″ mill.)

November 1985

"We're not going to see big reductions in the future — a few here and a few there. We have to do that in terms of competitiveness."[10]

—Jack Bollow
(U.S. Steel public affairs manager,
Mountain States area)

In mid-December 1985, U.S. Steel read Geneva's obituary by revealing that an agreement reached between U.S. Steel and a PoHang, Korea, steel plant will result in the closure of Geneva by 1989. A Brigham Young University professor predicted, however, that the plant would close much sooner than 1989.

Ruff Times

For Utah economic guru Howard Ruff, the 1980s have indeed been ruff times.

In 1979, Ruff foresaw "a runaway inflationary spiral" that would be followed by "an orgy of spending similar to what happened in Argentina when their inflation was running at 800 percent a year and they were buying everything in sight."[11] A Ruff ad in the May 1980 *BYU Today* warned: "The next three or four years could bring inflation rates higher than 50 percent." And, Ruff's 1981 book, *Survive and Win in the Inflationary Eighties,* featured this cover blurb: "Inflation will cause a Constitutional crisis before 1987."

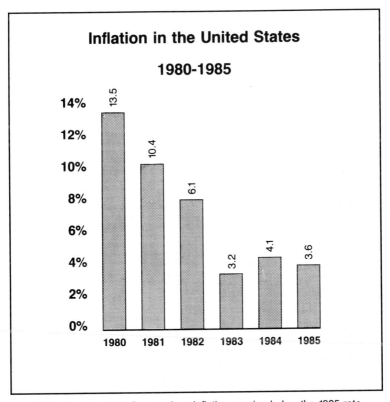

Inflation in the United States

1980-1985

NOTE: Early in 1986, figures show inflation running below the 1985 rate.

On inside pages of Ruff's book are found these forecasts for the 1980s:

"Lenders are becoming so gun-shy about rising inflation and interest rates that new fixed-rate, long-term mortgages will be dinosaurs by 1983."

"We will someday reminisce about the good old days of $2.00-a-gallon gas, and you had better plan your life accordingly."

"A recent prime rate of 21.5 percent [will cause us to look back] with nostalgia."

The book's back cover featured these forecasts for the 1980s:

"Gold will be over $2,000 an ounce and silver over $100."

"Rising gold prices will cause dividends from gold stocks to be greater than 1980 share prices."

"Interest rates will exceed 40 percent."

"Social Security pension benefits will exceed $100,000 a year — and still not be enough to live on."

"After 1982, there will be no more fixed-rate, fully amortized thirty-year home loans."

Forecasting the Great Depression

On October 24, 1929, prices on the New York Stock Exchange fell about $6 billion. Five days later, stocks plunged another $10 billion and proceeded irregularly downward for the next three years as America entered its worst economic depression.

"The statement that the present is a favorable time to get one's capital safely invested rests upon sound economic information."

"The number of economists and market students who are predicting a turn for the better in the bond market is steadily increasing."

—Advertisements,
  Salt Lake Telegram,
  October 23, 1929

"I believed we had reached a state where depressions and panics were a thing of the past. The American dream had been put on a sound statistical basis."[12]

—Marriner S. Eccles
*(Utah banker, head of the
Federal Reserve Board),
reflecting upon the 1920s*

"As we approach winter prosperity seems undiminished."

—Editorial,
*Salt Lake Tribune,
October 28*

"General business conditions are good...former precedents point to a recovery in the stock market which should continue at least until the end of the year."

—Advertisement,
*Salt Lake Tribune,
October 28*

"The worst that has been said about the situation is that it may reduce to a trifling extent the purchase of luxuries."

—Editorial,
*Ogden Standard-Examiner,
October 30*

"Bona fide stockholders will lose nothing."

—Editorial,
*Salt Lake Tribune,
October 31*

"The slump is about over and stocks have reached bottom."

—Advertisement,
*Salt Lake Telegram,
October 31*

This ad was published in the October 27, 1929, *Salt Lake Tribune:*

A Depression Myth

One of the great myths of Utah history relates to the Mormon "example" during the Great Depression.

We often hear that programs implemented by the LDS Church and its stakes effectively minimized the state's dependence upon federal welfare during the depression. Had other states followed the Mormon example by "caring for their own," the myth goes, the nation could have significantly reduced its dependence on New Deal relief.

Certainly, the Mormon aversion to government relief was well known at the time. An excellent expression of that philosophy was made decades earlier by apostle George Q. Cannon. When many states had appealed to the federal government to relieve crop losses caused by grasshoppers, Elder Cannon, noting that Utah also had suffered extensive grasshopper devastation, said:

> no begging appeal had gone up or out of Utah to other portions of the United States...we believe in assisting each other; and if our people lived in a State like Kansas or Nebraska they would be too proud to call for help from the rest of the nation because their crops had been destroyed one year. We believe in helping ourselves.[13]

But the Utah example of "gearing up" to avoid federal relief, especially during the worst depression years, was largely a fantasy. Nevertheless, it was reiterated as recently as April 6, 1986, in a *Church News* article:

> When the falling stock market signaled the plunge of the nation into the Great Depression in 1929, Church resources and ingenuity were marshaled by local and Churchwide leaders.

Some Depressing Statistics

Utah ranked in the top ten in virtually every statistical category of federal relief spending during the Great Depression.

"Utah would have blown away during the Great Depression except for federal relief; one in four Utahns was on direct relief. The state ranked second in per-capita volume of relief spent,"[14] said author Neil Morgan in a 1962 magazine article on Utah.

Morgan's comment likely refers to Utah's second place per capita ranking among the states in programs administered under the Social Security Act. These programs included old age assistance, aid to dependent children, and child welfare services. Instead of being "too proud to call for help from the rest of the nation," as Elder Cannon noted about earlier Utah, the state achieved a remarkable record in qualifying its needy citizens.[15]

By the end of June 1933, during the worst months of the depression, Utah ranked fourth in the percentage of families on federal relief. Only South Dakota, Arizona and Florida had a higher proportion of their population on welfare.[16]

A compilation of New Deal expenditures in Utah from March 1933 to September 1939, prepared by the Statistical Section of the Office of Government Reports, showed that Utah received a grand total of more than $289 million in federal assistance. Utah federal taxes for the same period were probably about $20 million.[17]

During the worst depression years, instead of "gearing up," the LDS Church actually "geared down" its charitable spending from more than $600,000 annually in the late 1920s, to $413,000 in 1933.[18]

According to Utah historian D. Michael Quinn, "The entire Church expenditure for relief that year [1933] was only one-third of the amount Salt Lake County spent on poor relief."[19]

Far from exhorting Church members to avoid government relief in the early depression, the Presiding Bishopric Handbook of Instructions urged members to turn to the county for relief before turning to the Church.[20]

Implementation of the Church Welfare Plan in 1936 had a comparatively insignificant impact in cutting Utah's dependency on government relief during the late Depression years. In fact, federal nonrepayable expenditures in Utah for the same years were ten times as great as the accountable value of churchwide Welfare Plan transactions.[21]

Expenditures for the period 1933-39 of the massive Federal Emergency Relief Administration ranked Utah eighth in the nation in per capita spending.[22] In the category, "Other Relief," Utah ranked fourth.[23] ("Other Relief" included clothing purchases for relief of the needy, Department of Agriculture relief programs, and other items.)

Utah's ranking in total federal expenditures per capita for the period 1933-1939 was ninth among the states.[24]

During the 1930s, when Utah was receiving high per capita amounts
of New Deal relief, President Franklin Roosevelt proved extremely
popular, capturing 69 percent of the state's popular vote in 1936.
Mormon President Heber J. Grant once lamented, speaking of Roosevelt,
"About half the Latter-day Saints almost worship him."

Certainly, the welfare picture in Utah has improved since the depression. Perhaps partially as a result of the expansion and increased effectiveness of the Mormon welfare program, Utah now ranks only 45th in percentage of residents receiving public assistance. Nevertheless, contrary to some reports, LDS leaders warn that if another Great Depression were to occur, Church welfare resources likely would be quickly depleted.

Christ Will Come in a Day or Two

In 1861, Joseph Morris claimed he had received revelations that Christ would come before the end of that year. As 1861 drew to a close, with his band of disaffected Mormons awaiting a visitation, Morris's revelations quoting the Lord became more frequent and more specific:

December 13

"I shall come up to you in the course of a day or two."[25]

December 22

"To have a correct faith they [the Morrisites] must believe that I shall not be more than two or three days at the farthest."[26]

December 28

"You may possibly see me on Monday. I may deliver my people on Monday; but if I should not come on Monday, I shall surely come on Tuesday; that you may depend upon."[27]

December 30

"I shall not wait more than two or three days under any circumstances whatever."[28]

December 31

"Let all my people settle up their accounts to-day, and prepare themselves for a visit from me to-morrow morning."[29]

Vital Statistics

"There are lies, there are damnable lies, and there are statistics," an obviously wise person once observed. As with other statistics, there is frequently more than one way to misinterpret vital statistics. Horror stories about Utah vital statistics have abounded for years.

Fiction: Utah's divorce rate is either the highest in the nation or close to it. In 1976, the president of the Equal Rights Coalition for Utah said, "Utah at present has the highest divorce rate in the nation."[30]

Fact: For decades Utah's divorce rate has been only slightly above the national average. Utah's rate of divorce is lower than any of its eight neighboring states and usually ranks between 20th and 25th nationally.[31]

Fiction: Utah has a high rate of illegitimate births among its teenagers.

Fact: Utah is almost always at or near the lowest among the 50 states in rate of illegitimate births. (Although Utah does have a high legitimate birth rate among teenaged mothers, when abortions are added to live births, the Utah teenage pregnancy rate falls dramatically in proportion to the rest of the country. This is because Utah abortion rates usually are the lowest in the nation.[32])

Fiction: Utah has a high per capita rate of drug abuse.

Fact: Utah has about half as many drug users per capita as the national average.[33] (Based on use analysis of marijuana, cocaine, heroin, and non-medical use of amphetamines, tranquilizers, analgesics, and sedatives.)

Fiction: Utah has a high rate of venereal disease.

Fact: Utah is usually at or near the lowest in the nation in this statistic. In 1985, Utah had 86.1 cases of gonorrhea reported per 100,000 population compared with a national average of 372.1 (both figures based on 1984 population estimates).[34]

Fiction: Utah has a somewhat more rural population than the rest of the nation.

Fact: Utah ranks seventh in the nation with an urban population of 84.4 percent, according to 1980 Census data.[35] Utah has a greater proportion of urban population than such "rural" states as Massachusetts, Connecticut, Pennsylvania, Ohio, Illinois, Maryland, and Michigan. (Population per square mile gives a much different picture, of course.)

Fiction: Due to the practice of polygamy, females outnumbered males in early Utah.

Fact: In every U.S. Census from 1850 to 1950, Utah males outnumbered females. Greatest disparities occurred in 1850 and in 1890 when the population was 53.1 percent male compared with only 46.9 percent female. By 1960, the proportion of males and females had evened out. The 1980 Census shows Utah females outnumber males by 50.4 percent to 49.6 percent. Based purely on numerical considerations, polygamy makes sense for the 1980s, especially for the United States as a whole where the proportion of females to males is now 51.4 percent to 48.6 percent.

Fiction: Utah has a high alcoholism rate. It is sometimes asserted that Utah's liquor law encourages drunkenness, for hardly anyone will go home with just a few drinks remaining in a bottle.[36]

Fact: Utah's alcohol consumption for the past several years was the lowest in the nation, based on per capita sales.[37] The number of heavy drinkers per capita is about half the national average.[38]

Fiction: Utah is among the leaders in suicide rates.

Fact: Utah's suicide mortality rate for the past five reporting years, 1980-84, was 13.2 per 100,000, compared with a national average of 12.1 and a Mountain States average of 17.0.[39] Dr. Harry Gibbons, director of the Salt Lake City-County Health Department, points out that Utah has a medical examiner system, whereas many states have coroners who are elected. Sometimes, Dr. Gibbons believes, coroners are reluctant to return a finding of suicide because "you just don't do that to friends."[40]

Those Dirty Movies

"Movies will get cleaner because that is the only direction they can possibly go."

—Harry Jones
  (Deseret News columnist),
  January 1, 1970

In 1978, when the University of Utah *Daily Chronicle* temporarily resumed printing ads for adult movies, the *Deseret News* editorialized:

> For many years now, the *Deseret News* has refused to run advertisements for X and R-rated movies...we don't mind expressing our regret that the "Chrony" got back into the business of advertising seamy films. But it's also encouraging to see this decision is still open to discussion and change.[41]

R-rated movie ads are now printed in the *Deseret News*. The one below appeared in August 1986.[42]

"A SHARP, SOPHISTICATED, FUNNY, SEXY, COMPASSIONATE PICTURE." —Jack Kroll, NEWSWEEK MAGAZINE

"RICHLY ENTERTAINING." —David Denby, NEW YORK MAGAZINE

MY BEAUTIFUL LAUNDRETTE

1986 Orion Pictures Corp.   ORION CLASSICS

NOW PLAYING! EXCLUSIVE ENGAGEMENT!   UTAH 148 South Main 328-2681   CHECK THEATRE GUIDE FOR SHOWTIMES.

First Impressions

In 1985, Dale Van Atta, a former *Deseret News* investigative reporter, was named to succeed Jack Anderson as "Washington-Merry-Go-Round" columnist. But judging by comments he made while editor of BYU's *Daily Universe,* Van Atta seemed to be the last person who would ever work for Anderson, let alone succeed him.

In an April 1972 article about Anderson, Van Atta said, "The man is more taken with his power than it would appear." The *Universe* editor worried about columnist Anderson's liberal leanings: "There is no Republican or conservative to challenge him in the public's eye." Anderson, said Van Atta, was sincere and convinced that what he was doing was right,

> yet sincerity has never been a great virtue in past personalities who believed that what they were doing was inevitably right. Take Hitler, for an extreme, or the thousands of persons who walk the line of sanity and insanity doing what they think "is right."

Quoting from *Capable of Honor,* Van Atta compared his future boss with people like Walter Wonderful:

> About themselves they drape the mantle of a terrible and terrifying righteousness, even as they engage in the most savage personal attacks upon those who disagree with them.

Anderson's column "could become dangerous for the country," Van Atta predicted.

In his conclusion, Van Atta observed Anderson might one day become like the man with the Muck-rake in *Pilgrim's Progress* "who was so concerned with raking filth from the ground that he could not see the celestial crown that was offered him."

Van Atta, considered by some to be the best investigative journalist in America, will never be accused of apple-polishing to get to the top.

Not to Worry

"Your best action is not to be worried about fallout."[43]

—Atomic Energy Commission booklet,
distributed to residents of St. George
at the time of Nevada nuclear testing,
1953

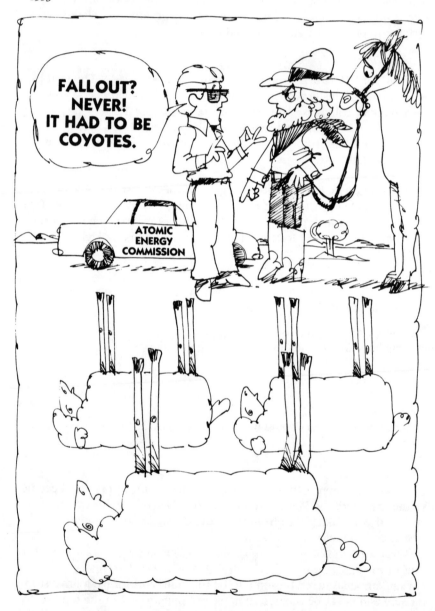

"Our experts have assured us that this sort of thing can't happen."[44]

—Joe Sanders
(Atomic Energy Commission official),
to ranchers showing signs
of radiation sickness,
1954

Grasshopper Kill "A Big Success"

June 15, 1985

Utah agriculture experts today called this spring's efforts to kill grasshoppers on heavily infested rangeland "a big success."[45]

June 24, 1985

"Grasshopper invasion called worst since 1933,"[46] declared a newspaper headline today. Grasshoppers in western Utah are devouring everything from rangelands to home gardens. A Clover area resident says her neighbors are now joking about baling grasshoppers instead of hay.

(Baling grasshoppers may not have been such a bad idea. A Virginia City, Nevada, newspaper in 1868 reported that Salt Lake City grasshoppers were being sold in Nevada grocery stores: "Those who are fond of crabs and shrimps will soon become equally fond of these nice, fat, Salt Lake grasshoppers."[47])

October 24, 1985

Governor Norm Bangerter declared Tooele County a disaster area as a result of the grasshopper devastation of last summer. Agriculture officials say Utah farmers lost far more than the $11 million damage from last year's invasion.

Ten Unusual People

Maurice Abravanel

"Lacks ambitions."[48]

—Edouard Abravanel
(Maurice Abravanel's father),
upon learning that his son
had quit medical school to
pursue a career in music.

Maurice Abravanel left New York in 1947 to take over the upstart Utah Symphony. By the time he retired in 1979, the symphony ranked among America's finest.

Dr. William DeVries

"You'll never amount to much."[49]

—high school principal
to student William DeVries

At the University of Utah Medical Center in 1982, surgeon DeVries implanted the first artificial heart in a human.

Don Lind

"The dreams that Utah's Don Lind had more than 20 years ago of flying to the moon will soon come true."

—*Ogden Standard-Examiner*
April 6, 1966

Astronaut Lind's dream of going to the moon has not come true. He did, however, make a space shuttle flight nineteen years after the *Standard-Examiner* offered this prediction.

Lee Provancha Day

"Give her piano lessons. She will never dance."[50]

—opinion offered by the family
  doctor after Lee, age nine, had
  a leg brace removed.

Lee Provancha Day performs in Ballet West production, "The Dream."

Debbi Fields

"Cookies? You want to sell cookies? Forget it."[51]

—Financial experts,
 *advising Debbi Fields in 1977 when
 she discussed with them the possibility
 of opening a cookie store.*

"Everybody told me I was going to fail."[52]

—Debbi Fields

"I thought it would fail."[53]

—Randy Fields
  (Debbi's husband)

Danny Ainge

"He will be another Brooks Robinson."[54]

—Pat Gillick
  (Toronto Blue Jays General Manager),
  1981

"He's not going to make a cent at pro basketball."[55]

—Richard Hoffer
  (Los Angeles Times writer),
  1981

"I've enjoyed my participation in pro baseball and feel I can compete on the major league level for a longer time than I could compete in basketball."[56]

—Danny Ainge,
  1980

Ainge, a lifetime .237 hitter, is now in his fifth year with basketball's Boston Celtics. He has recently negotiated a six year contract, effective in the 1986-87 season, said to be in the $700,000 per year range.

Ted Bundy

The comments which follow were made by friends, acquaintances, and co-workers of Ted Bundy who knew Bundy before the former Utah law student's proclivity for murder became generally known. They have been extracted from these publications: *Bundy: The Deliberate Stranger, The Only Living Witness,* and from *Utah Holiday's* series on Bundy beginning in October 1979.

"One of the nicest young men I have ever met."

"A nice, normal college student."

"He represented what it was that all young males anywhere ever wanted to be."

"I've always thought of you as a candidate for office one day. And a pretty good candidate, I'd guess."

"[Ted Bundy was] sort of Kennedylike."

"Obviously, he was someone who had a great deal of compassion in dealing with other people."

"He was the sort of person I would have trusted my life with."

"I wouldn't hesitate to line him up with my sister."

—comment attributed to
  a Mormon missionary

Dr. Willem J. Kolff

"Pure visionary."[57]

 This opinion of Dr. Kolff, a pioneer in the field of artificial organs, was offered by one of his colleagues at the Texas Heart Institute at about the same time Kolff was asking, "Why don't we make a total artificial heart?"

Reed Smoot

"Now that's a big lie. That's absolutely impossible. It couldn't be."[58]

—Reed Smoot

 As a small boy, Smoot offered this opinion when he heard Brigham Young predict that the human voice would be heard from New York to San Francisco. Ironically, many years later, as a U.S. senator, Smoot was invited to New York City to be the first man to speak over the completed coast-to-coast broadcasting system.

B. H. Roberts

"I'm going to win."[59]

—B. H. Roberts,
*assessing his chances of being seated
in the U.S. House of Respresentatives,
December 1, 1899*

 A month later the House voted 244 to 50 to exclude Roberts.

NOTES FOR CHAPTER 9

1. *Salt Lake Tribune,* May 1, 1976.
2. Ibid., May 5, 1976.
3. Ibid.
4. Ibid., January 14, 1977.
5. Ibid., September 9, 1977.
6. Ibid., December 16, 1977.
7. Ibid., January 10, 1978.
8. Ibid., March 10, 1978.
9. Ibid., December 6, 1978.
10. *Deseret News,* December 22, 1985 (refers to a November statement by Mr. Bollow).
11. Howard Ruff, *How to Prosper During the Coming Bad Years,* 1979, p. 15.
12. Marriner S. Eccles, *Beckoning Frontiers,* 1951, p. 52.
13. Journal of Discourses, Vol. 17, p. 337.
14. *Esquire,* August 1962.
15. Leonard Arrington, "Utah, The New Deal and the Depression of the 1930s," 1983, pp. 18, 24
16. Ibid., p. 11.
17. Ibid., p. 23.
18. Richard D. Poll, Thomas G. Alexander, Eugene E. Campbell, David E. Miller, *Utah's History,* 1978, pp. 484-485.
19. D. Michael Quinn, *J. Reuben Clark The Church Years,* 1983, p. 256.
20. Ibid., p. 257.
21. Poll, Alexander, Campbell and Miller, p. 488.
22. Don C. Reading, "A Statistical Analysis of New Deal Economic Programs in the Forty-Eight States, 1933-1939," doctoral dissertation, Utah State University, 1972, p. 140.
23. Ibid., p. 23.
24. Ibid., p. 140.
25. C. LeRoy Anderson, *For Christ Will Come Tomorrow,* 1981, p. 93.
26. *The Spirit Prevails,* (a compilation of writings and revelations of Joseph Morris), 1886, p. 315.
27. Ibid., p. 337.
28. Ibid., pp. 337-338.
29. Ibid., p. 341.
30. *Tribune,* October 24, 1976.
31. See Statistical Abstract of the United States.
32. "Teenage Pregnancy in Utah 1975-1981," Utah Department of Health, August 5, 1983.
33. "Alcohol and Drug Use and Abuse in Utah," Utah State Division of Alcoholism and Drugs, March 1985, p. 19.
34. Based on May 22, 1986, interview with representative of the Communicable Disease Bureau, Utah State Department of Health.

35. Statistical Abstract of the United States, 1984, p. 26.
36. *Harper's,* May 1980.
37. *Brewers' Almanac,* 1985.
38. "Alcohol and Drug Use and Abuse in Utah," Utah State Division of Alcoholism and Drugs, March 1985, p. 3.
39. Bureau of Health Statistics, Utah Department of Health, November 1, 1985 report.
40. *Tribune,* June 20, 1980.
41. *Deseret News,* May 1, 1978.
42. *Deseret News,* August 2, 1986.
43. John G. Fuller, *The Day We Bombed Utah,* 1984, p. 30.
44. Ibid., p. 91.
45. *Deseret News,* June 16, 1985.
46. Ibid., June 24, 1985.
47. *California Folklore Quarterly,* Vol. 5, 1946, p. 42.
48. Hope Stoddard, "Symphony Conductors of the U.S.A.," 1957.
49. *This People,* March 1983.
50. Ibid., August-September 1982.
51. *Esquire,* December 1984.
52. *Deseret News,* February 22, 1986.
53. *Esquire,* December 1984.
54. *Tribune,* March 25, 1981.
55. Ibid., March 30, 1981.
56. Ibid., September 19, 1980.
57. *Utah Holiday,* July 1982.
58. Bryant S. Hinckley, *The Faith of Our Pioneer Fathers,* 1956, p. 207.
59. Truman G. Madsen, *Defenders of the Faith,* 1980, p. 259.

Part 4

The U and the Y

Chapter 10

The University of Utah

A University Without Tuition

In petitioning the Legislative Assembly in February 1850, Brigham Young and other Utah leaders requested the creation of a territorial university that would be

> instruction free, so that the old and young, rich and poor, men, women and children throughout the State...may have the privilege of acquiring the most perfect education possible.[1]

Six weeks later, Chancellor Orson Spencer, in what is regarded as the university's official prospectus, echoed this sentiment: "No person will be denied the benefits of the University for want of pecuniary means."[2]

 The sentiment was noble, but beginning with the opening of classes on November 11, 1850, students have always paid tuition.

Salt Lake City — A Poor Place for a University

"A great city, like Salt Lake, is not the kind of place in which the youth of the rural districts and smaller towns of Utah can with entire safety reside during their two to five years of college life...

"The climate of Logan is excellent for hard study. Salt Lake has two months, October and May, during which the students grow languid and many of them get sick. This does not occur at Logan.''[3]

—J. H. Paul
(Utah educator),
explaining why the University of
Utah should be moved to Logan,
January 20, 1894

"[Near Fort Douglas] is no place for it. The proximity of soldiery is in
every way detrimental to the best interests of students. The immoral
atmosphere of such a place totally unfits it for the location of a university.
Besides, the place has no water and no electric facilities. It is away from
the city, and is a sage brush desert. Salt Lake cannot retain the Territorial
University by locating it on a dry, desert bench in the vicinity of a great
military post."

—*Logan Journal*
   November 22, 1893

Utah Not Big Enough for Two Universities

"Union is the only plan upon which this Territory can sustain a
respectable institution of higher learning."

—Editorial
   Deseret News,
   advocating combining the University of Utah
   with the Agricultural College at Logan,
   January 6, 1894

On August 18, 1894, the First Presidency of the Mormon Church also
took the position that Utah was not big enough for both a LDS Church
University and a Territorial University. The solution? Terminate the
Church University and encourage Mormons to send their sons and
daughters to the University of Utah:

Time has very plainly demonstrated the fact that Utah, while
abundantly able under present conditions to maintain one well
equipped institution for higher instruction, cannot adequately
support many such...the presiding quorums of the Church have
deemed it wise to bring the work of the Church University to
a close, that greater energy, resulting from concentration of effort,
may be devoted to the development of our Territorial University.
Toward the University of Utah our people may properly indulge a
feeling of pride...We recommend to the Latter-day Saints that they
faithfully devote their influence and energy, such as might have
been claimed by the university of the Church, had wisdom dictated

the continuance of that institution, to the University of Utah. We trust that our people will sustain the Territorial University by their good words and works, and particularly by their patronage in sending their sons and daughters who are prepared to become students in the institution...There appears no reason why our University should not become the great inter-mountain center for the diffusion of knowledge.[4]

The Curses of College Life

In 1902, the University of Utah *Chronicle* praised the faculty for eliminating math, sophomore English and physics as graduation requirements. The student newspaper called this move "the greatest god-send in half a century...[These subjects] have been the rocks on which many a student life has been wrecked or sadly damaged...they have been the curses of college life."[5]

Only one subject, freshman English, remained a requirement of all students.

Alas, the faculty giveth and the faculty taketh away. Only four years after the student "god-send," a faculty committee developed new, far stiffer graduation standards. Not only were English and math specified for entrance into the university program, but sixteen credit hours of foreign language were added. On top of this, six credits were mandated in each of four subject groups: physical science, biology and geology, history and political science, and social science and philosophy. English I remained a requirement.[6]

Unlikely Champions

Never was there a more unlikely national collegiate basketball champion than the University of Utah's 1943-44 squad.

Gaping holes were left in the school's schedule when several intermountain teams cancelled basketball because of the war. Utah likewise almost dropped basketball when it became apparent the team would be made up mostly of freshmen and that the schedule would consist primarily of second-rate opposition.

But the Utes went ahead, compiling a good enough record against their weak opponents to be extended an invitation to meet Kentucky in the first round of the National Invitational Tournament. To the surprise of no one, Kentucky eliminated the Utes, 46-38.

Normally, the season would have ended then. But an odd combination of misfortune and fortune yielded Utah a bid to the NCAA tournament which had commenced only a few days after the start of NIT competition. When the University of Arkansas basketball team suffered a death and two injuries in an auto accident, the Razorbacks withdrew from the NCAA tournament. The University of Missouri, originally the District 7 (Rocky Mountain region) representative in the NCAA field, was then named to replace Arkansas in District 6 (Southwest). Since Utah had been eliminated early from the ongoing NIT, the Utes were available and willing to accept the District 7 spot. This marked the first time in history a team had played in both the NIT and NCAA in the same year.

The decision to invite Utah, however, was not received enthusiastically by New York promoters. Based on Utah's inferior schedule and its poor showing in the NIT, promoters doubted that the Utes had any business showing up in Madison Square Garden.

Compared with getting there, competing in the tournament was a breeze. The underdog Redskins trounced one favored team after another to reach the finals against Dartmouth on March 28, 1944. Although one Dartmouth player had disparaged the Utes by suggesting that the Dartmouth team hold an intrasquad scrimmage before the game to give the fans their money's worth, Utah shocked the Eastern powerhouse 42-40 in overtime. To prove the victory was no fluke, two days later Utah whipped NIT champion St. Johns 43-36 to claim the undisputed national title.[7]

In the Rear No More

Salt Lake High School in 1899 crushed the University of Utah football team 34-0. The embarrassing defeat prompted this comment from the president of the University Athletic Association:

We have no reason to feel so sad over the crushing defeat lately received from the High School. When we but consider that they have been trained by an experienced instructor for two years, while we have had no teacher at all, it is no wonder that such a result came. No, we are not going to stop at that! If we are permitted a trained, thoroughly equipped, interested male teacher in gymnasium work and athletics, we shall never find ourselves in the rear again.[8]

The University got an athletic coach, Harvey Holmes, in 1900. But in 1903, the Utes suffered through a winless football season climaxed by a 17-0 loss to the Agricultural College at Logan. Criticism of the disastrous season was so severe that Coach Holmes resigned.

NOTES FOR CHAPTER 10

1. Ralph V. Chamberlin, *The University of Utah,* 1960, p. 5.
2. Ibid., p. 7.
3. *Deseret Evening News,* January 20, 1894.
4. Ibid., August 18, 1894.
5. University of Utah *Chronicle,* March 18, 1902.
6. Chamberlin, p. 256.
7. "Unlikely Champions" is based on March 1944 newspaper accounts of the Utes' postseason play.
8. *Chronicle,* February 7, 1900, cited in Chamberlin, p. 231.

Chapter 11

Brigham Young University

Growth

"If the present rate of growth continues, the studentbody will be 10,000 by 1960 and possibly 16,000 by 1970."[1]

—Ernest L. Wilkinson
(BYU president),
January 11, 1955

 At the time, some said this prediction was big talk. But Wilkinson turned out to be conservative. In 1970, BYU enrollment reached 26,689.

Academics

Half Truth: BYU is "Happy Valley," a great place to find a spouse, or to gain a testimony of the Mormon Church, or to watch football games. BYU cannot, however, compete academically with top U.S. universities.

Reality: BYU's academic standing does not yet rival its football rankings, but it's getting there.

During a recent four-year period, only Harvard, Yale and Princeton graduated more Rhodes Scholars than BYU.

BYU is one of only two schools that have ever placed three Danforth scholars in a single year.

The average ACT composite score of entering BYU freshmen in fall 1985 was 23.5, compared with a national average of 18.8.

BYU ranked 29th among higher education institutions in the number of entering Merit Scholars in 1985-86.

Acceptance rates of BYU students to professional schools are exceptional. BYU's medical school acceptance rate is 65 percent, compared with a national average of 47 percent. At dental schools, 92 percent of BYU students are accepted, compared with 70 percent nationally.

The J. Reuben Clark Law School, the Accounting Department, and other departments have been ranked among the finest in America.[2]

In 1985, *New York Times* education editor Edward B. Fiske and *Times* education writer Joseph Michalak offered this evaluation of BYU:

> BYU is as inexpensive as almost any private institution, cheaper than some of the publics, and academically competitive with the best of either.[3]

Those Unpredictable BYU Speakers

June 1954

In BYU's commencement address, Utah Congressman Douglas Stringfellow related a partial account of a cloak and dagger operation behind Nazi lines in World War II wherein Stringfellow led 200 soldiers on a foray resulting in the capture of Nazi atomic scientist Otto Hahn. Only five men returned from the daring adventure.

Although earlier in the year serious questions had arisen concerning the validity of Stringfellow's claims, the BYU audience was captivated by the stirring remarks of the man who many at the time considered Utah's greatest war hero.[4]

October 16, 1954

Congressman Douglas Stringfellow, speaking on KSL-TV, confessed that his story of heroism during World War II was a total fabrication and "a vicious lie."[5] Stringfellow was dumped by party leaders as the Republican candidate for Congress a few days later.

July 5, 1972

BYU President Dallin Oaks called upon student leaders not to allow BYU to be used as a platform for controversial speakers. "We're a mark for that sort of thing," he said. "The most important consideration is what moral position the person stands for."

Oaks said Dr. Henry Kissinger would not be invited to speak at BYU, for instance, because of Kissinger's playboy reputation.[6]

October 24, 1972

Vice President Spiro Agnew addressed an overwhelmingly receptive crowd of more than 20,000 at BYU's Marriott Center today.[7] The Nixon-Agnew ticket is so popular at BYU that if the election were held now, the result would be strictly "no contest."

October 10, 1973

"No contest," pleaded Spiro Agnew to charges of income tax evasion. Evidence gathered by U.S. attorneys shows that Agnew, who recently resigned the vice presidency, also solicited and received $100,000 in kickbacks while in elective offices.[8]

September 27, 1981

Former Secretary of State Henry Kissinger, visiting in Salt Lake City, attended a performance today of the Mormon Tabernacle Choir. Kissinger, winner of the 1973 Nobel Peace Prize, spoke to the choir following the performance.

"I would like to tell you how much I have admired you for all these years," he told the singers.

After his remarks, Kissinger was given a guided tour of Temple Square by leaders of the Mormon Church.[9]

Campus Crime

Myth: BYU's strict honor code, together with the university's affiliation with the Mormon Church, make it safe to presume that at BYU crime is something you hear happens at other universities.

Reality: Soaring larceny theft rates at BYU during the past few years have forced university personnel to post "High Theft Area" signs around campus.[10] A comparison of the University of Utah and BYU shows overall crime rates at BYU are much higher. (BYU student population in 1986 was 27,000; Utah, 25,000.)

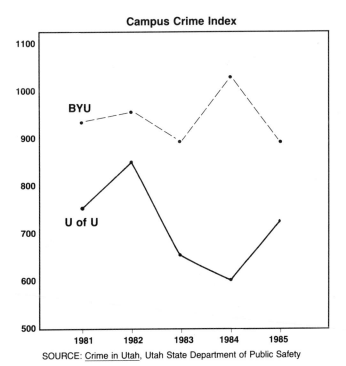

Campus Crime Index

SOURCE: Crime in Utah, Utah State Department of Public Safety

TOTAL PART I CRIME, 1981-1985
BYU 4720
UTAH 3562

Cougar Football — the Road to Number 1

Note: In 1898, the LDS Church Board of Education banned football at Mormon schools. The decision was rescinded in 1919.

"Football games are damaging to the respectability of such institutions and very destructive in their tendency of life, limb, and the religious tone that should always characterize every Latter-day Saint school of learning."[11]

—George Goddard
(general superintendent,
LDS Sunday Schools),
1897

"A barbarous, brutal exercise not to be dignified by the title of a game."[12]

—Karl G. Maeser
(president, Brigham Young
Academy, 1876-1892)

"I began to have doubts [in 1974] about our ability to produce a winning program."[13]

—LaVell Edwards
(BYU head coach, 1972-present)

"[BYU cannot be ranked higher] as long as the team is tied into several WAC games a year, against less-than-impressive opponents...BYU has gone about as far as it can go in the national rankings."

—John Mooney
(Sports editor, Salt Lake Tribune),
November 21, 1980
(BYU was ranked 13th at the time)

"But how soon will the Cougars play a schedule of 'name' opponents which would qualify BYU for contention for the national championship?

"The answer is, 'Not in the immediate future' unless BYU would elect to bolt the Western Athletic Conference and go independent, and that possibility appears very doubtful."[14]

—John Mooney
  September 16, 1982

"At last, BYU is in a rebuilding year."

—*Sports Illustrated,*
  picking BYU to finish 3rd in the WAC,
  September 5, 1984

"BYU will not win the national championship by playing in the Holiday Bowl."[15]

—Beano Cook
  (ABC-TV analyst),
  November 1984

"Even if BYU winds up the regular season unbeaten and untied and beats a good opponent in the Holiday Bowl, the chance of BYU being recognized as the national champion is slim."[16]

—John Mooney
  November 14, 1984

"BYU is ranked fourth in both wire service polls at 9-0, but could not possibly finish as No. 1 unless the nation experiences a series of earthquakes, floods and bubonic plague on selected campuses."[17]

—Jerry Izenburg
  (national sports columnist),
  November 1984

In early January 1985, BYU was voted number one in all major polls. Seven months later, a serious outbreak of bubonic plague decimated Wyoming's prairie dog population.[18]

Did BYU Deserve Number 1 Ranking?

When BYU finished the 1984 season ranked number one, many fans, athletes, and reporters around the country declared that the University of Washington, by defeating Oklahoma on New Year's Day, deserved the number one ranking.

"We're No. 1, no doubt."[19]

—Mark Pattison
(Washington wide receiver)

"Washington is the No. 1 team in the country."[20]

—Spencer Tillman
(Oklahoma halfback)

"They [Washington] deserve to be No. 1."[21]

—Barry Switzer
(Oklahoma head coach)

"I saw BYU play twice in 1984, and if that is the best team in America, the Pope is moving to Salt Lake City."[22]

—L. J. Swanson
Ft. Collins, Colorado

"If Brigham Young University is the best college football team in the country, Mickey Mouse is a duck. And everyone who voted for BYU is a quack."[23]

—Steve Love
(Knight-Ridder Newspapers)

"There's no excuse for having a university named after a polygamist, or one which cheated like hell to win, ranked ahead of (Washington)."[24]

—Student newspaper,
  University of Washington,
  January 1985

Nine months later, in a game many felt would decide once and for all which team really deserved the 1984 number one ranking, BYU crushed the University of Washington 31-3. It was Washington's worst football defeat since 1981.

The Missionary Edge

Years ago, when BYU football teams were perpetual losers, many fans, coaches, and reporters were sure BYU would never win consistently as long as players continued to interrupt their football careers for LDS missions.

In the late 1950s, Coach Harold Kopp lamented that he always seemed to have three teams: "One on the field, one in the hospital, and one on missions."[25] Coach Tommy Hudspeth observed that most football players, after returning from missions, "are really not too much interested in taking part in athletics."[26]

But times have changed.

In December 1985, Hawaii Coach Dick Tomey charged BYU with "an unfair advantage in maturity."[27] Coach Fisher DeBerry of Air Force agreed, "A twenty-three-year-old is just going to be more mature. They're more coachable, more stable."[28]

Recently, Coach LaVell Edwards said, "They used to say we couldn't win because of missionaries. Now they're saying we win because of missionaries...I wonder where all those people were when we were losing."[29]

BYU's national championship program in 1984 carried 52 returned missionaries.

Slow White Boys

Another excuse frequently given for BYU's football shortcomings before the Edwards era was the absence of black players in the speed positions: defensive secondary, receivers, and running backs.

In November 1968, amid protests over the race issue, San Jose State's black football players refused to play against BYU. San Jose State won 25-21 without them.

In the 1969 rematch, the black athletes returned. BYU won 21-3.

Also in 1969, fourteen black players refused to perform for the University of Wyoming in its October 19 game with BYU. Wyoming trounced the Cougars by 33 points.

A year later, Wyoming's black athletes played — BYU won by 20 points.

NOTES FOR CHAPTER 11

1. BYU *Daily Universe,* January 11, 1955.
2. Data provided by Wendell Evenson, BYU Associate Academic Vice-President, May 2, 1986.
3. *Deseret News,* December 15, 1985.
4. Frank H. Jonas, *The Story of a Political Hoax,* 1966, pp. 11-12.
5. Ibid., p. 7.
6. *Daily Universe,* July 5, 1972.
7. *Salt Lake Tribune,* October 25, 1972.
8. *New York Times,* October 11, 1973.
9. *Deseret News,* September 28, 1981.
10. *Tribune,* January 23, 1986.
11. Ernest L. Wilkinson and W. Cleon Skousen, *Brigham Young University, A School of Destiny,* 1976, p. 150.
12. *Cougar Illustrated,* November 2, 1985, p. 11.
13. LaVell Edwards, *LaVell Edwards,* 1980, p. 6.
14. *Tribune,* Setember 16, 1982.
15. *Deseret News,* November 3, 1984.
16. *Tribune,* November 14, 1984.
17. Ibid.
18. *New York Times,* August 9, 1985.
19. *Deseret News,* January 2, 1985.
20. Ibid.
21. Ibid.
22. *Deseret News,* January 13, 1985.
23. *Church News,* November 25, 1984.
24. Cited in *Deseret News,* September 15, 1985.
25. Gary James Bergera and Ronald Priddis, *Brigham Young University, A House of Faith,* 1985, p. 281.
26. Ibid.
27. *Deseret News,* December 10, 1985.
28. *BYU-National Champions,* 1985, p. 82.
29. Ibid.

Part 5

The Mormon Church

Chapter 12

Experts View Mormonism

The Church of Jesus Christ of Latter-day Saints, commonly known as the Mormon Church, is America's fastest growing native religion. Although antagonism toward the Church still surfaces occasionally, Mormons in the United States are generally considered patriotic, law-abiding citizens. With few exceptions, they receive favorable media attention for their commitment to family and religion.

It was not always this way, of course. Mormon founder Joseph Smith was accused of nearly every crime imaginable, from murder and infanticide, to having 500 illegitimate children. The early Church was defined by anti-Mormon writers as an "abortion," a "foul blot," and "a horrible deformity." This chapter consists of items based on early misperceptions of Mormonism beginning with the Utah era.

Slavery and Despotism

"Brigham Young rules with despotic sway, and death by assassination is the penalty of disobedience to his commands...[Mormons] are bound down by a system of church tyranny more complete than that which held the bondsmen of ancient Rome in the early days or now enthralls Africa's sons on the cotton fields of the South. The world has never seen a system of bondage, abject slavery, espionage and constant, unremitting tyranny in the most trivial relations of life more galling than that [with] which Brigham Young oppresses the people in the name of religion."[1]

—General Patrick E. Connor

Obviously, some Mormons were unafraid of risking "death by assassination." To a group which had disregarded his previous instructions, Brigham Young said: "You can do as you please. I have given so much counsel to the brethren...and have had it disobeyed, that I do not feel encouraged to counsel."[2]

Polygamy

Allegations of slavery in Utah were not limited to Church leaders ruling the territory with an iron hand. Prevailing opinion outside Utah during the last century also held that Mormon husbands enslaved women in polygamous marriages. As a by-product of this myth, Congress on August 4, 1886, appropriated $40,000 for a home in Utah to shelter "thousands of polygamous wives seeking escape from their cruel husbands who treated them like Moslem slaves."[3]

Funds for the shelter were also appropriated in 1888, 1890, and in 1891.

The shelter attracted so few women that it was soon turned over to the Territory for use as a school for the deaf and dumb. Average shelter population was only 14 women.

One New York newspaper depicted Utah as a "Cave of Despair" for women.

According to another polygamy myth, Brigham Young and other prominent Mormon polygamists had only the vaguest notion of how many wives and children they actually had. Young, on more than one occasion, was said to have inquired the name of a youngster, only to find the child was his own.

In *Roughing It,* Mark Twain, tongue-in-cheek, quotes Brigham Young as saying:

> I built a bedstead seven feet long and ninety-six feet wide. But it was a failure, sir. I could *not* sleep. It appeared to me that the whole seventy-two women snored at once. The roar was deafening. And then the danger of it! That was what I was looking at. They would all draw in their breath at once, and you could actually see the walls of the house suck in.[4]

 Twain reversed his digits — Young had 27 wives, not 72.

On April 24, 1870, Reverend J. P. Newman, preaching to his congregation in Washington. D.C., with President Ulysses S. Grant in attendance, got so carried away in denouncing polygamy that he declared it "an abomination in the sight of the Lord and *prohibited by the Bible.*"[5]

 Many Old Testament prophets practiced polygamy.

Flooding Utah With Bibles

One scheme to overthrow Mormonism was the American Bible Society's effort to flood Deseret with Bibles. It was presumed that if the territory were submerged with Bibles, Mormons would stop reading the Book of Mormon and drift away from their church.

> This campaign foundered when it was discovered that there were more Bibles per residence available and more Bible reading per capita in Utah than anywhere else in the country, and that unmistakable Hebrew sanction for polygamy was found in the Old Testament.[6]

Mormon leader John Taylor offered this comment on the effort:

> The Bible Society got up a report about two months ago, that they
> were going to send a Bible agent to Utah. We then hastened to
> offer them our cooperation, but as we advanced to receive the
> precious gifts, they vanished into their original element — gas![7]

The Decline of Mormonism

To help the reader better appreciate the statements which follow, the
graph below is provided.

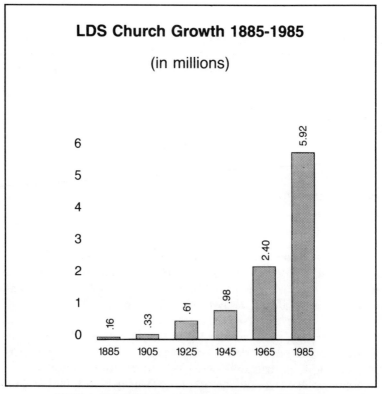

LDS Church Growth 1885-1985

(in millions)

Year	Value
1885	.16
1905	.33
1925	.61
1945	.98
1965	2.40
1985	5.92

NOTE: In May 1986, Church membership passed 6 million.

"[Joseph Smith] never could succeed in establishing a system of policy which looked to permanent success in the future."[8]

—Thomas Ford
(former governor of Illinois),
1854

"The Mormon rulers take great pains to have it believed that their community is continually and rapidly increasing. This, however, is a very great mistake. There has always been a curious state of accumulation and loss going on with them, and the loss is at present probably the largest part of the account. There is no society in the world in which there are so few permanent members, in proportion to the converts originally made. Many of the newborn Saints very soon lose the soda-water enthusiasm which is first experienced, and fall away; many, who have zeal enough to commence the mighty pilgrimage toward the modern Zion, cool off, and lodge like drift-wood by the way. Each emigrating body tapers off, something like the army of Peter the Hermit in the first great crusade...[Mormonism is like] a miniature whirlwind upon a dusty plain [which grows swiftly] until it somewhat suddenly subsides...it needs no great degree of prophet-sagacity to foresee its [Mormonism's] subsidence in like manner."[9]

—Benjamin Ferris
(former Secretary of the
Utah territory),
1856

"Once the general detestation and hatred pervading the whole country against the Mormons is given legal countenance and direction, a crusade will start against Utah which will crush out this beast of heresy forever."[10]

—*San Francisco Daily Evening Bulletin*
1857

"Though it would be rash to assume that Mormonism is dead, it would be equally rash to believe it can survive, for any extended period, the death of its great leader."[11]

—*Indianapolis Sentinel,*
following the death
of Brigham Young,
1877

"The Mormon church was stronger at four o'clock Sunday afternoon than it ever will again become; the remarkable will and organizing force of the dead leader departed with him, and have been transmitted to none other in his church; and we may now watch with complacency, if not with joy, the gradual disintegration of the whole Mormon fabric."

—*Salt Lake Tribune,*
  following the death
  of Brigham Young,
  1877

"The click of the telegraph and the roll of the Overland stage are its [Mormonism's] death rattle now. The first whistle of the locomotive will sound its requiem; and the pickaxe of the miner will dig its grave."[12]

—Samuel Bowles
  (editor of the Hartford Times)

"By encouraging the influx of Gentile population...in the course of a decade, the Mormon ascendancy would be destroyed...and the great octopus, shorn of its political power, would be obliged to assume its proper station among the ranting sects which come and go and are forgotten.[13]

—George Seibel
  (author, The Mormon Problem),
  1899

"I think Mormonism is doomed, sooner or later — the sooner the better... this foul blot [Mormonism] upon our civilization shall be known only as a horrid night mare of the past — this 'hideous she monster' shall retire to the black caverns of hell from which she came.

   "God grant it may be so!"[14]

—Reverend Edgar Estes Folk
  (author, The Mormon Monster),
  1900

Later Mormon Population Forecasts

"The True Church cannot ever be proportionately larger than it is today."[15]

—Bernard DeVoto
 (American editor and critic),
 1930

"We can safely forecast a Mormon population of...more than five million by the turn of the century. When that time comes, there will undoubtedly be more than a thousand stakes and five thousand wards."[16]

—Senator Wallace F. Bennett
 1958

 In 1986, there were six million members, 1600 stakes, and 13,000 wards and branches in the Church.

"Dr. Arthur L. Beeley, dean emeritus of the Graduate School of Social Work at the University of Utah, believes the influx of industrial population will reduce the proportion of Mormons in Utah by 1970 from about 65 percent to as little as 35 or 40 percent."[17]

—*Esquire*
 August 1962

 By 1970, the Mormon population of Utah had increased to 72 percent.

Angel Moroni was Black, Says Professor

Dr. Elmer Wells, an associate professor at the University of Southern Colorado, wrote a thesis in 1977 attempting to prove that the Book of Mormon prophet Mormon and his son Moroni were blacks.

To back up his claims, Dr. Wells pointed to origins of names containing the root "mor." He said that persons with such names have Moors or other Africans as ancestors. Wells also maintained that the hieroglyphics on the golden plates which the angel Moroni presented to Mormon founder Joseph Smith represent "the language of an ancient black African people."

"The inscriptions on the plates were written in hieroglyphics, which is nothing less than a European name for the language used by the early black Africans," Dr. Wells said.[18]

Follow the Leader

It is often observed that, since Mormons consider their top leaders to be prophets, Church members will automatically follow their counsel, like sheep. (As one writer said, "If you got ten Jews in a room, you'd have forty different opinions. Well, if you get ten Mormons in a room, you'll have one opinion."[19]) While the following three case studies certainly are inadequate by themselves to dispel this view, they do suggest the "blind obedience" phenomenon may be overrated.

Grant Goes Zero for Four

During the 1930s, Mormon President Heber J. Grant tried on at least four occasions to influence Utah voters.

In 1932, he made a preelection statement that he was voting for and supporting Senator Reed Smoot. Smoot, who had been considered unbeatable up until that time, lost. Grant in 1932 also endorsed Herbert Hoover, the losing Presidential candidate in Utah and in the nation.

The following year, Grant made frequent appeals for Church members to vote for retention of prohibition. On November 7, however, the state voted by a three to two margin to replace national prohibition, and two to one to repeal the state's prohibition law. Apostle Joseph Fielding Smith, writing in 1959, noted that Utah cast the decisive vote against national prohibition:

> Utah, contrary to the wishes of the General Authorities of the Church, joined with the majority of the states in demanding repeal, and the Beehive State held the doubtful, if not disgraceful, position of being the thirty-sixth state of the Union to hold a constitutional convention and thus brought about ratification of repeal.[20]

Ironically, at this time, the Mormon Church was marking the 100th anniversary of the Word of Wisdom, the Church's revelation against "strong drink" and other harmful substances.

No quitter, Grant in 1936 again tried his luck at influencing Utah voters, who by this time were receiving large sums of New Deal welfare assistance. Before the election, he said his great hope was that Governor Alf Landon would defeat Roosevelt in November. But the President carried nearly 70 percent of the Utah vote.

Speaking of Roosevelt, Grant once remarked that "about half the Latter-day Saints almost worship him."[21] (See cartoon, page 102) The Mormon leader personally felt Roosevelt was a cheat and a liar.

McKay and Nixon

On October 12, 1960, Mormon President David O. McKay endorsed Richard Nixon for president "as a Republican and a personal voter." McKay received considerable criticism for making such an open declaration of support. It was felt McKay's endorsement would give Nixon an even greater edge among Utah voters.

A closer analysis of the 1960 election results shows this was not the case.

In 1956, the Republican Presidential candidate (Eisenhower) received 65 percent of the Utah vote. In 1960, however, Nixon received only 55 percent, a 10 percent decline. This decline was the largest Republican drop in the eight-state Rocky Mountain region. Naturally, it is impossible to say positively why the state voted that way. But if McKay's statement had any effect at all, perhaps it helped Kennedy.

(In 1868, Brigham Young had no better luck then McKay. Utah voters elected a popular bishop as a write-in candidate in a local race over the Church president's own nominee.)

Hunting Deer for Sport

On the eve of deer season in 1978, President Spencer Kimball, in a general conference talk, spoke against hunting deer for sport.

"Now," said Kimball, "I also would like to add some of my feelings concerning the unnecessary shedding of blood and destruction of life…It is not only wicked to destroy them [wildlife], it is a shame, in my opinion."

In comments that mentioned deer specifically several times, Kimball quoted President Joseph F. Smith:

> If they [deer and antelope] should wander out of the park, beyond the protection that is established there for these animals, they would become, of course, an easy prey to those who were seeking their lives. I never could see why a man should be imbued with a blood-thirsty desire to kill and destroy animal life…I do not believe any man should kill animals or birds *unless he needs them for food.*

A national news story later asserted there is little need to hunt deer for food since, when all hunting related expenses are figured in, it is almost always less expensive to purchase supermarket meats.

Did Utah deer hunters, the majority, presumably, Mormons, follow President Kimball's recommendation? Records of the Utah Division of Wildlife Resources[22] show that in the three hunting seasons preceding Kimball's talk, there were 162,541 bucks taken in Utah. In the three years following the talk, the buck harvest jumped to 183,175. In the latter period, hunting license issuance increased by 33,000. (This comparison is of the regular license buck harvest. There were no regular harvest doe licenses issued in the period studied, 1975-80. In 1974 and before, regular doe licenses were issued.)

NOTES FOR CHAPTER 12

1. Leonard Arrington, *Brigham Young, American Moses,* 1985, p. 296, and E. B. Long, *The Saints and the Union,* 1981, p. 215.
2. Arrington, p. 178.
3. Wayne Stout, *History of Utah,* Vol. 1, 1967, p. 436.
4. Mark Twain, *Roughing It,* 1872, p. 125.
5. Samuel W. Taylor, *The Kingdom or Nothing,* 1976, p. 239.
6. Truman G. Madsen, *Defender of the Faith,* 1980, p. 249.
7. Taylor, p. 179.
8. Thomas Ford, *History of Illinois,* 1854, pp. 354-355, cited in B.H. Roberts, *Comprehensive History of the Church,* 1930, Vol. 2, p. 347.
9. Benjamin G. Ferris, *Utah and the Mormons,* 1856, p. 322.
10. Cited in Robert B. Day, *They Made Mormon History,* 1968, p. 282.
11. Cited in Taylor, p. 12.
12. Ibid., p. 225.
13. George Seibel, *The Mormon Problem,* 1899, p. 88.
14. Edgar Estes Folk, *The Mormon Monster,* 1900, p. 284.
15. Bernard DeVoto, "The Centennial of Mormonism," from *The American Mercury,* January 1930.
16. Wallace F. Bennett, *Why I Am a Mormon,* 1958, pp. 166-167.
17. *Esquire,* August 1962.
18. Pueblo, Colorado, *Chieftan,* July 6, 1977.
19. *Sunstone,* September-October, 1981, comment attributed to Peter Bart, author of *Thy Kingdom Come.*
20. Joseph Fielding Smith, *Essentials in Church History,* 1959, p. 645.
21. D. Michael Quinn, *J. Reuben Clark, The Church Years,* 1983, p. 69.
22. Utah State Division of Wildlife Resources, "The 1982 Utah Big Game Harvest Book," p. 16.

Chapter 13

Tall Tales

Mormon leaders have long been concerned about the proclivity of Church members to circulate tall tales having spirtual overtones. Elder Harold B. Lee in 1964 lamented, "It never ceases to amaze me how gullible some of our Church members are."[1] To some extent, the Church has successfully used mass communications to dispel tall tales. Still, old habits are hard to break.

Following the 1978 decision to give the Mormon priesthood to all worthy males, speculation circulated that LDS leader Spencer Kimball had received a personal visit from Joseph Smith, or from the Lord, or from other heavenly messengers directing the change. But Kimball made no such claims. He explained that the decision was made gradually, after prayer, and after consulting with other Church leaders.

Early in 1986, a caller to a Salt Lake area radio show said, "a friend told me that President Benson fainted while receiving a vision which will be given to the world soon."[2] In reality, the Mormon leader's fainting episode occurred as a result of standing up too quickly, a fact duly noted in Utah media.

Another incident surfacing in 1986 was the distribution of a letter in Utah and elsewhere stating that the president of Proctor and Gamble admitted on a TV program to being a disciple of the devil. The Proctor and Gamble product logo, a man in the moon looking at three stars, was said to be a symbol of the devil. A KSL-TV editorial called the letter "drivel," and a LDS Church statement in May asked members not to circulate the false story.

This chapter consists of ecclesiastical trash and faith-promoting fairy tales originating within the Mormon Church which have since been junked.

The Horseshoe Prophecy

This prophecy was supposedly received by President John Taylor while in Cedar City. In his vision, recorded by Edward Lunt, Taylor "saw war in Salt Lake City...so great was the destruction of life within the city that blood ran down the gutters as though it were streams of water." The only means of leaving the terrible destruction would be by foot, and the people would fight so vigorously among themselves that it would become necessary "to remove the Church records across the Colorado River."[3]

Some in the Mormon Church speculated that blood would run in the gutters after an attack by angry blacks on Salt Lake City. (This speculation naturally originated long before the 1978 revelation allowing blacks to hold the priesthood.) Perhaps in partial corroboration of the big black attack theory, a *New York Times* survey in 1972 found that one-third of Mormons believed there was a black conspiracy to destroy the Mormon Church.[4]

A First Presidency letter in 1970 said this about the Horseshoe Prophecy: "This is just another evidence of the cleverly designed motives of individuals who seize upon the emotionalism of our present day to get publicity."[5]

The White Horse Prophecy

According to the White Horse Prophecy, the Prophet Joseph Smith used these words to describe the LDS Church in the Rocky Mountains: "The White Horse will find the mountains full of minerals and they will become very rich. You will see silver piled in the streets...You will see gold shoveled up like sand."[6]

Joseph, according to the prophecy, also saw war in the nation but peace "only in the Rocky Mountains."

In a 1918 general conference address, President Joseph F. Smith said the White Horse Prophecy "was never spoken by the prophet in the manner in which they have put it forth. It is simply false; that is all there is to it." So that his listeners would be sure not to miss the point, Smith called the prophecy "a lot of trash."[7]

Did an Old Mute Lead the Pioneers?

Some claimed that an elderly mute guided the pioneers across the plains:

> In the van of this army, on the march to Utah, was often seen a venerable man with silver beard, who never spoke, but who would point the way whenever the pilgrims were faint or discouraged. When they reached the spot where the temple was afterwards built, he struck his staff into the earth and vanished.[8]

... or was it Joseph Smith?

"Joseph Smith, as a resurrected being, guided Brigham Young across the plains and led him to Utah."[9]

—John Musser
(fundamentalist Mormon)

"When Joseph Smith migrated west and founded Salt Lake City..."[10]

—Dr. Elmer Wells
(associate professor, University of Southern Colorado)

Did Joseph Smith Ever Make it to Utah?

"Lorin Woolley said that the bodies of Joseph and Hyrum Smith were dug up, put in new caskets, and brought to the Salt Lake Valley at a very early date. Lorin further stated that the bodies were buried in the Salt Lake temple grounds."[11]

—Charles W. Kingston
(fundamentalist Mormon)

 The bodies of Joseph and Hyrum Smith are at Nauvoo, Illinois. They were not moved across the plains.

Hail to the Chief

A story entitled "The Coming of the Great White Chief," written in 1945 by Norman C. Pierce, received wide circulation for years among Mormons. A summary of the tale:

In southern Mexico is a secluded and beautiful walled city of the White Chicaraga Indians. The city has remained untouched and unspoiled by the evils of civilization since it was built long before the time of Christ. These Indians, having deep blue eyes, dress in long white robes which have symbolic marks which they regard as very sacred. The Indians abstain from tobacco and liquor and have a set of records written in a language they no longer speak. Many years ago there was a great storm with fearful earthquakes and thick darkness for several days. After the darkness was lifted, a Great White God descended to them from the heavens. This God stayed for a short time, teaching the Indians how to live. Once each year the Great White Chief calls his followers to a great annual conference where he presides over and teaches them. The Indians have implemented a great welfare plan. In 1940, the Great White Chief told his followers the time had come to build a magnificent temple. At this time (1945), 20,000 Indians are now cutting and polishing stones of white marble. They will then migrate north to build a great temple and a beautiful city within a wall.[12]

Pierce attributed his story to an Indian named Natoni Nes Bah. In 1953, the Church asked Bah if the story were humbug. His reply: "I have read the story written by Norman C. Pierce entitled 'The Coming of the Great White Chief' ... There is no truth in this story."[13]

As late as 1966, this tale was still being circulated, causing the Church to issue a priesthood bulletin reminding members that it had been repudiated many times.

Latter-day Disappearing Acts

The Book of Mormon teaches that three descendants of ancient American peoples, called Three Nephites, were allowed to "tarry" or remain on the earth, similar to the apostle John in the New Testament. In the LDS Church, there have been many reports of appearances by one or more of these Three Nephites. As with UFO sightings, it is virtually impossible to determine which reports of Three Nephite appearances may be legitimate and which may be, in the words of apostle Anthon H. Lund, spiritual manifestations caused "by an overloaded stomach."[14]

A BYU professor tracked down one such story to its source:

> Bill learned from Dave of a couple who picked up a man while
> they were on their way to the temple. The man warned of the
> need to get in a year's supply of food right away, then vanished.
> Dave got the story from a girl he knew. The girl heard it from a
> man in good standing in her ward. The man received it from a
> very close associate in his ward. This close associate heard it from
> a friend who owns a wholesale gas business and delivers gas to the
> farmers. A housewife on a farm where the gasman delivered gas
> related it to the gasman during the course of a delivery. The
> housewife said her son and his wife had told her about it. That
> couple got the account from their small daughter who heard it
> from one of her classmates in kindergarten.[15]

And Many Shall Starve

President David O. McKay, purportedly, received this vision in 1966:

> I have just had a vision and many in Salt Lake will die this very
> winter. It will come upon them so fast that they will not have time
> to prepare and many will starve to death.[16]

When McKay told of this vision, he was said to have tears in his eyes.

When it was discovered that the alleged vision was news to McKay, Church officials ordered the fabricator of this story to stop publishing it. The man persisted and was excommunicated.

When the Lord Comes

In an April 1970 general conference address, First Presidency
counselor Harold B. Lee discussed two myths then being circulated.[17]

Concerning claims that some know that there are people alive today
who will see the Savior when he comes, Lee said: "This again is fictitious."

About the notion that one of the general authorities has been told he will preside over the LDS Church when the Savior comes, Lee declared: "This is, of course, false."

Elvis Presley and the Mormons

During the early 1970s, a story was circulated at BYU that Elder Paul H. Dunn of the First Quorum of Seventy had personally visited with Elvis Presley, that the two discussed the Mormon Church, and that Elvis was quite interested.

According to Elder Dunn, it didn't happen:

> The fact is...that Merrill Osmond was discussing with me at one time the possibility of talking with Elvis Presley and that Elvis and he had conversed a little bit about the Church. Merrill Osmond had hoped that I could meet with Elvis at some future time. That meeting never took place.[18]

Chameleonic Pigmentosa

Before LDS President Spencer Kimball in 1978 announced that worthy blacks would be allowed to hold the Mormon priesthood, Caucasian Church members often reported that faithful dark-skinned Mormons were becoming whiter and whiter. Even the Church's Relief Society President, Belle Spafford, detected this chameleonic transformation:

> I've seen some of those dark-skinned Indian children who had been in the [Indian Placement] program. After a few years, [they] look as if they were more white than Indian.[19]

Since 1978, chameleonic pigmentosa has been on the wane. As if to underscore this, a passage in the Book of Mormon (2 Nephi; 30:6) referring to a "white" people was changed by the Church in 1981 to a "pure" people, comforming to an early edition of the Book of Mormon.

NOTES FOR CHAPTER 13

1. *Improvement ERA,* June 1970, p. 64.
2. Heard by the author on his car radio, January 13, 1986.
3. "A Prophecy By President John Taylor," as told by Edward Lunt, no date, copy at LDS Church Library, Salt Lake City.
4. *New York Times,* April 6, 1972.
5. *Church News,* April 14, 1970, p. 3.
6. "Visions of the Latter Days," published by Ogden Kraut, no date, pp. 8-12, copy at LDS Church Library, Salt Lake City.
7. Conference Report, October 1918, pp. 57-58.
8. Charles M. Skinner, *Myths and Legends of Our Own Land,* Vol. 1, 1896, p. 72.
9. J. Max Anderson, *The Polygamy Story: Fiction and Fact,* 1979, p. 93. (Musser attributed this comment to Lorin C. Woolley who attributed it to President John Taylor.)
10. Pueblo, Colorado, *Chieftain,* July 6, 1977.
11. Mark J. Baird and Rhea A. Baird, *Reminiscences of John W. Woolley and Lorin C. Woolley,* Vol. 3, p. 25.
12. Norman C. Pierce, "The Coming of the Great White Chief," 1945, copy at LDS Church Library, Salt Lake City.
13. *Church News,* May 16, 1953.
14. Thomas G. Alexander, *Mormonism in Transition,* 1986, p. 297.
15. Dr. Duane E. Jeffery, used by permission. Cited in Don. L. Penrod, "Critical Analysis of Certain Apocryphal Reports in the Church of Jesus Christ of Latter-day Saints As Related By Members of the Church," BYU master's thesis, 1971, pp. 27-28.
16. Penrod, p. 29.
17. *Improvement ERA,* June 1970, p. 64.
18. Paul H. Dunn, letter to author, May 2, 1986.
19. Robert Gottlieb and Peter Wiley, *America's Saints,* 1984, p. 174.

Chapter 14

LDS Second Thoughts

Chapter 14 consists of two sections. Statements highlighted in the first section, "Winds and Doctrines," include views which either are not now accepted by the Mormon Church or which are under debate. The second section, "Meet the Mormons," consists of second thoughts and erroneous predictions about prominent Mormons.

Note: As a result, perhaps, of the Mormon belief in modern revelation, some Church members are perfectly content to ascribe virtual infallibility in doctrinal matters to LDS leaders. But the leaders themselves seem more cautious: "We are not infallible in our judgment, and we err," said President J. Reuben Clark.

Winds and Doctrines

"Jesus was the bridegroom...We say it was Jesus Christ who was married ...I shall say here, that before the Savior died, he looked upon his own natural children, as we look upon ours."[1]

—Orson Hyde
  (apostle),
  discussing the marriage of
  Cana of Galilee

"The thought is becoming almost universal in the British Isles, that Israel [the Ten Tribes] is there, where we have always known them to be."[2]

—Anthony W. Ivins
  (counselor in LDS First Presidency)

"I believe in plural marriage as a part of the Gospel, just as much as I believe in baptism by immersion for the remission of sins...Can I afford to give up a single principle? I can not. If I had to give up one principle I would have to give up my religion."[3]

—George Teasdale
(apostle),
January 13, 1884

 Although the Church gave up plural marriage in 1890, Elder Teasdale did not give up his religion.

"Brigham [Young] pointed out that God was a developing being still in the process of growth — still progressing in knowledge and wisdom."[4]

—Leonard Arrington
(Mormon historian)

"It should be realized that God is not progressing in knowledge, truth, virtue, wisdom, or any of the attributes of godliness...[Those who believe this are] intellectuals without strong testimonies...[they] will live and die weak in the faith."[5]

—Bruce R. McConkie
(apostle)

"He [Adam] is our Father and our God, and the only God with whom we have to do."[6]

—Brigham Young

 This concept, never accepted by the Church, came to be the basis of the "Adam-God" theory.

"There will not be any temple finished until the one is finished in Jackson county, Missouri, pointed out by Joseph Smith."[7]

—Brigham Young

 In 1986, the LDS Church had 40 temples in operation throughout the world, but none in Missouri.

"There are many here now under the sound of my voice, probably a majority, who will have to go back to Jackson County and assist in building the temple."[8]

—Lorenzo Snow
 (Mormon Church president),
 November 7, 1900

"The Roman Catholic Church...[is] most abominable above all other churches."[9]

—Bruce R. McConkie

"There is no harmony between the truths of revealed religion and the theories of organic evolution."[10]

—Bruce R. McConkie

"Widstoe left little doubt of his belief that the Holy Spirit directed evolutionary changes."[11]

—Thomas G. Alexander
 (historian),
 discussing John A. Widstoe, a
 Mormon apostle and scientist

"The theory of organic evolution is a product of good science. It is a powerful, well-substantiated tool for explaining many facts and observations in nature. Numerous LDS scholars find [the theory of evolution] both scientifically sound and not in conflict with God's revelations...To the LDS scientist...[evolution] is an expression of God's omnipotent control of nature — not beyond law but fully in accord with it."[12]

—Lester Allen
 (scientist, former BYU dean)

"It is doubtful that man will ever be permitted to make any instrument or ship to travel through space and visit the moon or any distant planet.

"The Lord will permit men to go just so far and no farther...All this talk about space travel and the visiting of other worlds brings to mind vividly an attempt long ago made by foolish men who tried to build to heaven."[13]

—Joseph Fielding Smith
(apostle, later Church president),
1958

"A worse set of ignoramuses do not walk the earth...I could put all the real knowledge they possess in a nut shell and put it in my vest pocket, and then I would have to hunt for it to find it."[14]

—Brigham Young
on doctors

Although Young, on another occasion, said, "I see no use for them [doctors] unless it is to raise grain or go to mechanical work,"[15] he eventually encouraged the study of medicine.

"To sit among them [lawyers] is like sitting in the depths of hell, for they are as corrupt as the bowels of hell...Keep away from court houses; no decent man will go there unless he [is compelled]."[16]

—Brigham Young

Young later urged thousands of young and middle-aged men to study law. He was certainly not the last Utahn ambivalent about lawyers. On October 15, 1978, a poll showed that 55 percent of Utahns lacked confidence in lawyers.[17] Only three months later, another poll said 72 percent of Utahns felt lawyers were doing a fine job.[18]

"If there were some need — which there is not! — to single out one member of the Godhead for a special relationship, the Father, not the Son would be the one to choose."[19]

—Bruce R. McConkie,
explaining why no one should talk of
developing a "special relationship" with Christ,
1982

Subtitle: "Deepen our personal relationship with Jesus Christ."
Conclusion: "Establishing a personal relationship with the Savior promises deep joys both here and in eternity."

—LDS Relief Society,
  Spiritual Living Lesson #5,
  1979-80

Blacks and the Church

Note: On June 9, 1978, President Spencer Kimball announced that all worthy males, regardless of race, would be allowed to hold the Mormon priesthood.

"How long is that race to endure the dreadful curse that is upon them? That curse will remain upon them, and they never can hold the Priesthood or share in it until all the other descendants of Adam have received the promises and enjoyed the blessings of the Priesthood."[20]

—Brigham Young

"If the white man who belongs to the chosen seed mixes his blood with the seed of Cain, the penalty, under the law of God, is death on the spot. This will always be so."[21]

—Brigham Young

(No wonder Tommy Hudspeth, while football coach at BYU, said: "We have certain rules and regulations which we won't change; we will not allow inter-racial dating."[22])

"The Lord decreed that the children of Cain should not have the privilege of bearing the Priesthood until Abel had posterity who could have the Priesthood, and that will have to be in the far distant future. When this is accomplished on some other world, then the restrictions will be removed."[23]

—Joseph Fielding Smith

"Negroes in this life are denied the priesthood; under no circumstances can they hold this delegation of authority from the Almighty."[24]

—Bruce R. McConkie

"It has been the doctrine of the Church, never questioned by any of the Church leaders, that the Negroes are not entitled to the full blessings of the Gospel."[25]

—The First Presidency
August 17, 1951

"When one hears the Tabernacle Choir, one forgets that no Negro could ever hope to achieve a place in that group."[26]

—Wallace Turner
(author, The Mormon Establishment)

 Blacks performed with the choir even before the priesthood revelation.

"Few expect, however, that Spencer Kimball will receive the necessary revelation."

—*Time*
January 14, 1974

Contrary to some reports, not all pre-1978 LDS leaders believed blacks would have to wait until the next life to receive the priesthood:

"I felt he [David O. McKay] would have changed the doctrine had he kept his health and vigor in his later years. Hugh B. Brown assured me a change was coming."[27]

—Lowell L. Bennion
(Mormon scholar, community leader)

"[J. Reuben Clark] recommended 'preparatory' priesthood quorum organization and training for persons of African Negro identity because he firmly believed they would one day receive the priesthood during this life."[28]

—D. Michael Quinn
  (Mormon historian)

"There is not now, and there never has been, a doctrine in this Church that the Negroes are under a divine curse. We believe that we have scriptural precedent for withholding the priesthood from the Negro. It is a practice, not a doctrine, and the practice will someday be changed. And that's all there is to it."[29]

—David O. McKay
  (Church president),
  1954

Meet the Mormons

Heber J. Grant

"The laziest boy in the Thirteenth Ward."[30]

—Bishop Edwin D. Woolley

 Grant, while president of the Mormon Church, once said:

> I assert with confidence that the law of success, here and hereafter, is to have a humble and prayerful heart, and to work, work, WORK...I do not know of anything that destroys a person's health more quickly than not working. It seems to me that lazy people die young.[31]

Spencer W. Kimball

"[I was] the laziest boy that ever lived, especially in that generation... Where there was work to do, I could always find a shady place to sit down and dream."[32]

—Spencer W. Kimball

"She predicted that within six months Spencer would apostatize."[33]

—This 1928 prediction by an acquaintance
*of Kimball was made after Kimball had
chosen a salaried Church position over
a "spiritual" calling.*

 In 1973, Kimball became the 12th president of the Mormon Church.

J. Reuben Clark

"I think there is no more danger of my being named [an apostle] than there is of my flying to the moon."[34]

—J. Reuben Clark
May 19, 1931

"You can't get him, Heber, because he is a $100,000 a year man."[35]

—Anthony W. Ivins
*(first counselor to LDS
President Heber J. Grant),
discussing with Grant whether J. Reuben
Clark might be available to serve in the
First Presidency,
1931*

 Clark became second counselor to Grant in 1933.

Dallin H. Oaks

"I was the dumbest boy in third grade."[36]

—Dallin Oaks

 Formerly president of BYU and a Utah State Supreme Court justice, Oaks now is a Mormon apostle.

Paul H. Dunn

"Class, I have taught English in this school for over thirty years, and without a doubt this is the dumbest boy I have ever had."[37]

—English teacher,
evaluating student Paul Dunn

 Paul H. Dunn has been an LDS general authority since 1964. Once a professional baseball player, Dunn is an educator, a prolific writer, and a favorite speaker with Mormon audiences.

Belle Spafford

"You may not last that long, Sister."[38]

—J. Reuben Clark,
responding to Belle Spafford's inquiry in 1945
about whether she could expect to serve a "customary"
five-year term as Relief Society president.

 Mrs. Spafford lasted a record 29 years.

Susa Young

"I have no desire to be any man's wife. And doubt whether I ever shall."[39]

—Susa Young
(daughter of Brigham Young),
1879

 In 1880, Susa Young married Jacob Gates. Later, she wrote of every girl that "in her secret soul she really looks forward to marriage as the one desirable thing in her life."[40]

LeGrand Richards

"[It's] only a matter of hours [before LeGrand Richards dies]."[41]

—Attending physician
March 2, 1979

 The following week, Elder Richards attended a meeting of the LDS Quorum of the Twelve and said, "I read in the minutes where you'd received word of my imminent demise, but I fooled you, didn't I?"[42]

Richard P. Condie

"You're too old."[43]

—David O. McKay
(Mormon president),
responding to Condie's request to be
made permanent conductor of the
Mormon Tabernacle Choir,
1957

 Condie prevailed and served 17 years a conductor. In 1957, Condie was 59; McKay 83.

Mormon Tabernacle Choir

"We can't sing with this great choir and have it come over a little kitchen radio."[44]

—Anthony C. Lund
(Tabernacle Choir conductor),
1929

 Sound reproduction was excellent for the choir's first network radio broadcast on July 15, 1929. The choir has been doing network broadcasts ever since.

NOTES FOR CHAPTER 14

1. Journal of Discourses, Vol. 2, p. 82.
2. Conference Reports, October 3, 1926, p. 18.
3. Journal of Discourses, Vol. 25, p. 21.
4. Leonard Arrington, *Brigham Young, American Moses,* 1985, p. 207.
5. Bruce R. McConkie, *Mormon Doctrine,* 1966, p. 239, and *Sunstone Review, April 1982.*
6. Journal of Discourses, Vol. 1, p. 50.
7. B. H. Roberts, *Comprehensive History of the Church,* 1930, p. 136.
8. Thomas G. Alexander, *Mormonism in Transition,* 1986, pp. 288-289.
9. McConkie, *Mormon Doctrine,* 1958, p. 139.
10. Ibid., p. 238.
11. Alexander, p. 275.
12. Gary James Bergera and Ronald Priddis, *BYU, A House of Faith,* 1985, p. 170.
13. Joseph Fielding Smith, *Answers to Gospel Questions,* Vol. 2, 1958, pp. 191-192.
14. Arrington, p. 310.
15. Ibid., p. 311.
16. Journal of Discourses, Vol. 3, pp. 240-241.
17. *Salt Lake Tribune,* October 15, 1978 (Utah Poll).
18. Based on KUTV "Extra" survey which aired January 19, 1979. Cited in *Utah Holiday,* February 1979.
19. *Sunstone Review,* April 1982.
20. Journal of Discourses, Vol. 7, pp. 290-291.
21. Ibid., Vol. 10, p. 110.
22. Bergera and Priddis, p. 299.
23. Wallace Turner, *The Mormon Establishment,* 1966, p. 231.
24. McConkie, *Mormon Doctrine,* 1966, p. 527.
25. John L. Lund, *The Church and the Negro,* 1967, p. 89.
26. Turner, p. 244.
27. *Sunstone,* February 1985.
28. D. Michael Quinn, *J. Reuben Clark, The Church Years,* 1983, p. 233.
29. Pamela R. Taggart, *Mormonism's Negro Policy: Social and Historical Origins,* 1970, p. 74. (Comment attributed to McKay by Sterling M. McMurrin.)
30. Russell R. Rich, *Ensign to the Nations,* 1972, p. 486.
31. Heber J. Grant, *Gospel Standards,* 1941, p. 183.
32. Edward L. Kimball and Andrew E. Kimball, Jr., *Spencer W. Kimball,* 1977, p. 38.
33. Ibid., p. 170.
34. Quinn, p. 37.
35. Ibid.
36. *This People,* August-September, 1982, p. 27.
37. *This People,* Summer 1981, p. 34.
38. *Dialogue,* Summer 1971.
39. Ibid., Autumn 1983.
40. *Young Woman's Journal,* January 1897, p. 183.
41. Lucile C. Tate, *LeGrand Richards: Beloved Apostle,* 1982, p. 295.
42. Ibid.
43. Charles Jeffrey Calman and William I. Kaufman, *The Mormon Tabernacle Choir,* 1979, p. 101.
44. *Tribune,* July 8, 1979.

Post Script — Great Predictions

Those who read *Drat! Mythed Again* might receive the mistaken impression that the author thinks no one ever makes a correct prediction. I include, therefore, the following good predictions I stumbled over while searching for the other kind.

"I heard recently of a city that the outsiders are endeavoring to start, called Corinne, which it is said is to be the great city of the interior West...there may be a rush there, for a short time, of speculators, loafers, and rowdies...but it will soon die out, and the people be scattered to some other places."[1]

—Daniel H. Wells
(counselor to Brigham Young),
April 7, 1869

"I think, however, our town will eventually become a good football town."[2]

—Harrison R. Merrill
(BYU sports publicist),
1922

From a Texas newspaper in 1953:

BENSON REALLY HAS 'CONTACTS'

"Secretary of Agriculture Ezra Taft Benson apparently has contacts that are literally out of this world. When Benson left San Antonio on Sunday, he promised south Texas farmers and ranchers immediate drought aid.

"Less than 24 hours later it rained for the first time in months."[3]

"Should Clay [later Muhammad Ali] last the distance or beat the champion, you'd hear the cry of 'fix' from here to Washington, D.C."

—John Mooney
(Salt Lake Tribune *sports editor*),
February 24, 1964

(The next day, Mooney's counterpart at the *Deseret News,* Hack Miller, gave this assessment of Clay's shocking victory over heavyweight champion Sonny Liston: "Obviously a fix or a phoney.")

"It is hard to tell people just how big this game is to us."[4]

—LaVell Edwards
(BYU head football coach),
October 29, 1974

(When Coach Edwards made this comment about the upcoming Arizona game, BYU was 2-3-1, and appeared well on the way to continuing a tradition of football mediocrity. But BYU won, trouncing the 14th-ranked Wildcats in Tucson, 37-13, and went on to finish 7-3-1, qualifying for the Fiesta Bowl. The football program at BYU hasn't been the same since.)

"As a news anchor, Sullivan handles her assignment well. Does this mean she will join the ranks of other ex-4's?"

—*Mountainwest*
January 1979

(Not long afterward, Kathleen Sullivan left Channel 4. She can now be seen on ABC national news.)

"Ainge Could Be BYU's Edge In Tonight's Game Vs. Irish"[5]

(The above headline ran in the *Salt Lake Tribune* on the day of Danny Ainge's now legendary full-court dash against Notre Dame in 1981 which brought BYU a 51-50 NCAA tournament victory. BYU had trailed by 14 points in the second half.)

"He's elusive on that."[6]

—Sterling Webber
(Salt Lake mayoral candidate),
October 1983

(Webber was suggesting that Mayor Ted Wilson, if reelected, would not serve out a four-year term. Wilson resigned in 1985 for other employment after serving only a year and a half of his third term.)

"It's not a question of if Geneva will be shut down, but when."[7]

—Warner Woodworth
(professor in BYU School of Management),
November 16, 1984

(Thirteen months later, U.S. Steel announced the phaseout of operations at Geneva.)

"...chances are good they'd get the same treatment Ted Kennedy got from Jimmy Carter — they'd get their rears whipped."

—LaVarr Webb
(Deseret News political writer),
discussing Republican chances in the 1985
"non-partisan" Salt Lake mayoral race,
May 1, 1985

(After a promising early showing, the Republicans lost big.)

"Utah is a long shot."[8]

—Calvin L. Rampton
(Utah governor),
assessing Utah's chances of
winning the 1972 Winter Olympic bid,
April 18, 1966

(Although many at the time had predicted Utah would be selected to host the games, Rampton gave this note of caution. Utah finished last in the balloting.)

NOTES FOR POST SCRIPT

1. Journal of Discourses, Vol. 13, pp. 24-25.
2. *BYU Today,* October 1984.
3. Ezra Taft Benson, *Cross Fire,* 1962, p. 128.
4. *Salt Lake Tribune,* October 29, 1974.
5. Ibid., March 19, 1981.
6. Ibid., October 24, 1983.
7. *Deseret News,* November 16, 1984.
8. *Tribune,* April 19, 1966.

ILLUSTRATION CREDITS

page 6,   Utah ski photo, courtesy Salt Lake Convention and Visitors Bureau

page 14,   Finley and Harris maps, courtesy Utah State Historical Society

page 26,   Thistle, courtesy Utah Department of Transportation

page 38,   Adam S. Bennion and J. Bracken Lee, courtesy Special Collections, University of Utah Marriott Library

page 79,   1952 and 1983 Salt Lake City floods, courtesy Utah State Historical Society

page 89,   Cougar Stadium, courtesy Brigham Young University

page 111,   Lee Provancha Day, courtesy Ballet West, photo by Mark Wagner

page 144,   "The Cave of Despair," courtesy University of Utah Press, reproduced from *The Mormon Graphic Image, 1834-1914*

Index

The Author

Steve Warren has won numerous writing awards including three first places in statewide contests. His writing has appeared in local, regional and national publications.

He has a B.A. degree in communications.

An Oregon native, Mr. Warren and his wife Ja Niece reside in West Valley City, Utah. They have two children.

Additional copies of *Drat! Mythed Again* are available by sending check or money order for $10.95 plus $1.50 for postage, handling and sales tax to Altair Publishing, P.O. Box 20024, West Valley City, Utah 84120. Subtract $1.50 per book on orders of two or more books.